A War Baby

Rags to Riches

by

Tom Grainger

**Grosvenor House
Publishing Limited**

Text updated and amended August 2010

Tom Grainger is hereby identified as author of this
work in accordance with Section 77 of the Copyright, Designs
and Patents Act 1988

The book cover picture is copyright to Tom Grainger

This book is published by
Grosvenor House Publishing Ltd
28-30 High Street, Guildford, Surrey, GU1 3HY.
www.grosvenorhousepublishing.co.uk

A CIP record for this book
is available from the British Library

ISBN 978-1-907211-46-1

Acknowledgments

My youngest daughter Kate asked me on several occasions to record my life story for the benefit of the grandchildren and posterity She inspired this book after I had declined several times but was I was finally persuaded to put pen to paper, and was further encouraged after several people outside the family who read the original draft told me that I must get it published. Whilst the exact accuracy of all events and dates cannot be taken as Gospel I have made every effort to record the story as accurately as my memory will allow. All of the names are or were living people who had a great influence on my life and the narrative has been recorded, as I believed it to be true.

Thanks are due to many people for their help in the compilation of this book, with dates and facts that had to be slotted into place, firstly to my family, as I could rarely remember my children's birthdays let alone the grandchildren's. To all MMF, Selkirk and Rite Vent staff, both past and present. Thanks to Joanne and Richard, for their help in setting up the website and printing draft copies of the manuscript. Jack and Katie, my two eldest grandchildren, for teaching me how to use a desktop publisher, and to friends, relatives and business associates who have also made useful contributions and are still a source fond memories. Last but by no means least. Grosvernor House Publishing Ltd., who guided me through the mysteries of getting my first book to press.

Foreword

Having been totally captivated by Tom's fascinating book I feel that I have been on a truly privileged tour into the past, into quite amazing settings and been accorded such a rare insight into the hugely interesting lives of many. And our excellent Guide is, of course, author Tom, a total gentleman of the highest integrity, of supreme wit and humour with a splendid talent for writing in such an attractive manner. It's difficult to leave the book once you've begun. We feel that we are utterly present with Tom in experiencing the very real lives of his family and neighbours before, during and post-Second World Wartime England.

We witness "Monday morning washday, which began with a small galvanised bath being placed over two gas rings of the cooker. When it was hot enough it was poured into the Tub. Next the Dolly Maid, pounding away at the washing, for very dirty overalls the washboard, a scrubbing brush and Red Carbolic or Sunlight Soap was the answer." How those images evoke such precious memories for so many!

We follow Tom through an amazing life experience that knew poverty, ill health and having to leave school at the age of fifteen. The inspirational support of his wonderfully determined mother provided him with such uplifting self-esteem, energetic enthusiasm and created a true man of great vision who bravely confronted many challenges in such a cheerful, courageous and optimistic manner. Ultimately, Tom reached richly deserved success in business.

He felt so blessed to have met, through real Irish good luck, his beloved wife, Joan Healy from Millstreet, Co. Cork. Little did Tom realise the significance of the name "Clara" in his life when in 1938 he was born at No. 2, Clara Place in Birmingham and would later in life meet with someone so very special who lived close to the famous Clara Mountain near Millstreet! Family life is so beautifully presented to us in Tom's own inimitable writing style. Readers cannot but so love his witty approach. To whet the appetite – let us listen to how Tom describes an acquaintance who was not over-generous: ".....(this particular gentleman) had deep pockets and short arms where money was concerned..."! Or again when describing Wartime England: "Street Cred was not an issue in those days - to have any sort of car on a council estate, elevated the family to snob status..."!

There is so much more to share about this true gem of a book but I shall not delay you any longer from beginning your own superb tour with your excellent Guide, Tom. I recently had the privilege of meeting with Archbishop Bernard Longley of Birmingham at a wedding in London. He, like Tom, has such a very genuine feeling for the importance of one's own place. Both gentlemen are supreme Ambassadors for their great city of Birmingham. We are indeed fortunate here in Millstreet to have become acquainted with our wonderful Friend, Tom Grainger, of such generous spirit, who was so marvellously discerning to have chosen Joan, a Millstreet lady of the highest calibre as his wife and the mother of his splendid family.

It has been such an honour to have been requested by Tom to introduce the second edition of his true masterpiece "A War Baby – Rags to Riches". We truly look forward to many more books from Tom ..... and film rights can be discussed in time!

Seán Radley,
Curator, Millstreet Museum
and Local Broadcaster   24th August 2010

This book is dedicated to the memory

of

Claire and Joan

The Author

An autobiography tracing the life of a baby boy that was born into poverty in a back street area of Birmingham, just before the outbreak of World War II, who suffered with ill health during the early part of his life and had little education leaving school at the age of fifteen. With the help and determination of his mother, whose unceasing belief in him, drove him onwards and upwards and although the climb towards success had many setbacks. He meets and falls in love with an Irish girl from County Cork, which brought with it the luck of the Irish and four delightful daughters. An astute business brain brought him wealth, but sadly tragedy followed with the death of his wife and a daughter within three years of each other.

Me aged Six

Most of Tom's creative work is now done in Sutton Coldfield, Warwickshire, and Cloughoula-More, Millstreet Town, County Cork, Ireland

www.Tomgraingerbooks.com

Contents

CHAPTER ONE

The Early Years

House number 2 Clara Place, back of 312, Cooksey Road, Small Heath, Birmingham, was a very inauspicious and humble home to await my arrival on 20th July 1938. My mother described me as a tiny, wizened, screeching mite, but with all of the love that only a mother can give, she christened me Thomas William Grainger, the fourth generation of first sons to bear that name.

I was called Tommy, to avoid confusion with my father Tom and I was very fortunate to have been born in July, a summer month as 2/312 Cooksey Road was close to the bottom of the social housing spectrum and at that time, did not enjoy electricity or a bathroom and the only means of heating was an open fire, when coal was available. If I had not managed to discard my potty before I left Clara Place, I would have shared a toilet with several other families at the bottom of the yard. This could be very inconvenient if neighbours chose to study the Racing Gazette while passing the time of day.

If this was not bad enough the country was still recovering from the Wall Street Crash in America which had resonated across the world, causing mass unemployment for more than a decade so on a personal level meant that my father was in and out of work at a time when social benefits were something for the future. My birth had also been difficult for my mother Lillie, who had to be hospitalised in the Women's Hospital Loveday Street, not just causing gynaecological complications, but the additional anguish of how the hospital bill would be paid. It would be several years later in 1948 that the free health service came into being.

My sister Constance, or Connie as she was known, had been born three years earlier in Dudley Road Hospital, in May 1935 and with my arrival, and the whole family living together with my Grandmother, it qualified us for one of the new council houses, which were being built in Erdington - to be precise number 51 Chipstead Road. Things were starting to look up for me, this was not just a council house, it was a home with electricity, a bathroom and toilet and three bedrooms. All for seven shillings and sixpence per week rent and rates. We had no central heating, but a back boiler behind the open fire was able to produce hot water for our baths and washing.

Our house was mainly furnished with my Granny Bowdler's furniture from Cooksey Road, it was always kept clean and well cared for. My indoor play area in the living room was a wooden floor covered with lino and occasional hand made mats and a small kitchen, which had a red quarry tiled floor, regularly mopped by Grandma. An old piano and china cabinet were the luxuries that survived the move. The china cabinet is still treasured today in a bungalow in Ireland.

However, I was oblivious to the fact that all was not sunshine and roses. Dark clouds and worrying news was arriving daily from Europe. Early in 1938 Adolph Hitler with his Nazi Party in tow, had taken over Austria, without a shot being fired and by October of the same year, he was preparing to attack Czechoslovakia. The First World War had only ended two decades before and memories of the atrocious loss of life were still vivid in the minds of my parents. I was only fifteen months old when Germany invaded Poland leading the then, dithering Prime Minister, Neville Chamberlain, to declare that Britain was now at war with Germany.

As England prepared for war, the unemployment situation improved almost overnight. Manufacturing and in particular the automotive industry, which was very strong in the Midlands, was turning its attention to increasing production of military vehicles, aircraft and ammunition so more lesser paid jobs became available.

Dad was very lucky to get a job as a tram driver, very lucky indeed as it turned out, as transport was considered to be an essential service for conveying workers to the munitions' factories and he was prevented from being called up for active service, which possibly saved his life.

His employment as a tram driver earned him the princely sum of £3 seven shillings and six pence a week at a time when there were 240 pennies to the pound, this gave our family £3 plus Granny's widow's pension to feed, clothe and meet other every day expenses, after the rent had been paid. My Dad was based at Witton Tram Depot, which was almost opposite the Witton Road Stand at Villa Park, the home of Aston Villa Football Club. He worked many different shifts both days and sometimes nights. As well as being a driver he would also be expected to help with cleaning and basic maintenance work on the trams, in addition to being a member of the Home Guard when not working.

My father had been very bright at school and was the eldest son of eight children, with three younger brothers and four sisters. His school had offered his parents a scholarship for Grammar School, but his father, also called Tom, was a very strong, left wing, Trade Union shop steward, and had refused, saying that his son was needed to work, to help support his younger brothers and sisters. This left my Dad with very little ambition in life.

He was a man with many talents; he gave up learning the piano after only three lessons, but an exceptional ear for music enabled him to play the piano by ear at any party, wedding or pub if a piano was available. He was also amazing at mental arithmetic and could have given Carol Vorderman a run for her money, if she had been around then. His lack of ambition remained and throughout his life, he worked hard manually and was quite content, as long as he provided enough for his family to live on. He was a very caring and loving father, and left my mother to correct us whenever we were mischievous.

My mother, Lillie Grainger (nee Bowdler), was almost opposite in character, she was short in stature, but long in ambition. She was the youngest child having an older sister Emma and an older brother Jim, who all were ambitious go-getters, or movers and shakers, as they would be known today. She had married my father at St Oswald's Church Bordesley on the 16th June 1934 only four months after her own father James, had died quite suddenly, with previously undiagnosed bowel cancer. His widow, Emma Bowdler, was to play a substantial role in moulding my character until her death on 21st June 1952, shortly before my fourteenth birthday.

Mum's opportunity to increase our family income was enhanced early in 1940, when she was given the chance to do her part for the war effort by working at the Nuffield's factory at Castle Bromwich, which was then engaged in the manufacture of Spitfire fighter planes. Hence the Spitfire Island near B&Q on Chester Road, which remains as a monument to the part it played in the defence of Britain.

Mum's day began early at 6am when she would walk to Shortheath Road to catch the No28 bus to Castle Bromwich and after a day's work in the aircraft factory; she would not arrive home until we were ready for bed at 6.30 in the evening, often working on Saturdays as well. This meant that my sister and I were brought up, or minded by day, by our Granny Bowdler, a tall, stout woman who was caring, and would spoil us with little treats, but would also stand no nonsense.

At this time, we all had ration books, and rationing was causing long queues at the shops. My Granny was very good at producing delicious food and dinners from anything that was available. On one occasion, she provided dinner and pudding for us, both made from sausages and dried apple rings. The sausages became 'Toad in the Hole' and the remaining batter, with the dried apple rings on top, became our pudding. On other days, she poured golden syrup on the cooked batter, which was also one of my favourites. Vegetable hot pots and rabbit stews were also special dinners that I looked forward to, other days our dinner may have been fried battered SPAM with POM dried potato. Another treat was when any stale bread was soaked in water and together with dried fruit and limited other ingredients, became delicious bread pudding. Nothing was ever wasted; a virtue that still lives with me today, very often to the mirth of the rest of my family.

If any food was left over or waste food had gone off, it would be taken to pig bins, which were on every street corner, so that any waste food could be collected daily to feed pigs at any nearby farms. All iron railings and any other surplus metal was removed and collected for production of weapons. Our flowerbeds were dug up, and potatoes and other root vegetables were grown, and we were all asked to make a personal contribution to beating the Germans. My uncle Jim had a car but he was unable to get any petrol for private use, but I did see some cars and vans with flexible gas containers fitted to the roof of these vehicles.

Meanwhile, we were being looked after by Gran, who was also doing all of the jobs about the house. Monday morning was always washday. She would start by putting a small galvanised bath over two gas rings of the cooker and when the water was hot enough, she would pour it into a galvanised tub she would then add soap flakes and start to work with the Dolly Maid, pounding away at the washing. For Dad's very dirty overalls, she would use the washboard, a scrubbing brush and Sunlight or red carbolic soap. After swilling all the clothes in cold water, she would put the wet clothes through the mangle, to remove as much water as possible, before hanging them out on the washing line.

Many children in the industrial towns were being evacuated to rural locations, which were well illustrated recently by the archival film footage of pathetic disorientated children, complete with gas masks on a cord around their necks, being herded onto trains or charabancs to unknown destinations in bewilderment as to what lay in store for them. I should also add that the destinations were very difficult to find, due to the removal of signposts and town names in anticipation of an invasion, possibly by enemy soldiers being parachuted in. All of these factors conspired together to make it very difficult for these small children to have much contact with parents who were working long hours, not to mention the restriction on travel, and the telephone being a device rarely seen by ordinary people.

Mum told us that she would not allow us to be evacuated, and then cheered us all up by saying that if a bomb struck our house we would all go together. I would listen for wailing sirens' warning of the approach of German aeroplanes, I also heard the droning engines of lots of bombers in the sky, both by day and night, not knowing whether they were passing overhead, or if they were going to bomb us in Birmingham. Later on they would only bomb us at night, Mum told us that the Spitfires that she helped to make were shooting the German planes down in daylight and after that, the planes would only come to bomb us at night. When I was taken to the shops I could see big balloons in the sky, Mum said they were barrage balloons and stopped low flying aircraft. At night, looking out of my bedroom window, I could see high-powered searchlights shining high into the sky, with a criss cross of beams searching for the German bombers, to help our ack-ack gunners to shoot them down.

Our family was similar to others in the road, as we dug a big hole in the back garden near to the house where Uncle Jim and the neighbours all joined in to help us erect a corrugated iron Anderson shelter on a concrete base. When it was finished it was half underground and then they mixed more concrete and poured it on top, before covering it with the earth that had been dug out of the hole. The shelter provided a small opening at the front for us to get in. Inside there were four metal bunk beds, bottles of water and a first aid kit with wooden splints and bandages. We thought that this was very exciting, and the idea of camping out in a tin shed was an adventure to look forward to. However, because of the damp, spiders and creepy crawlies, Mum and Dad would only let us use it when the bombing was very close. Most nights we slept on a mattress under the stairs which Mum said was the safest place. One night my sister Connie was crying when a bomb shook the house, and I told her not to worry as Mom's Spitfires would save us, such was my blind faith in my mother as a small boy.

By September 1939 over one and a half million Anderson shelters had been distributed with good effect. On November 14th 1940 Coventry was almost totally destroyed in a seven hour Blitz by German Aircraft, more recently analysed on a BBC documentary, on the 70th anniversary of that dreadful night.

My Dad was also a member of the Home Guard, so brilliantly portrayed by 'Dad's Army' and whilst very humorous by the casting of the characters, the Home Guard together with the ARP (Air Raid Precautions) were both compulsory organisations that played a vital role in fire watching and policing the blackout regulations, which ensured that no light was exposed and thereby provide any navigational help to the enemy. Training was also given in search and rescue and extinguishing the fires caused by incendiary devices, which could be widely scattered.

We heard on the news that our soldiers had been evacuated from Dunkirk by lots and lots of small boats, and Mum told me that my Uncle Peter was one of the Desert Rats and was fighting the Germans in North Africa, and that he only escaped capture by swimming two miles when the Germans captured El Alamein.

My Uncle Jim, Aunt Gladys, and my cousins, Iris and Ray, were bombed out of their house in Bodesley Green and after a short stay with his sister's family, came to live at number 31 Chipstead Road, only just down the road from us. We were delighted that our cousins would be near us to play and Jim would also be near his mother. Uncle Jim had his own business. He was a Cabinet Maker, but had also taken on furniture upholstery as well, in his factory in Sheepcote Street, off Broad Street, Birmingham. His sister Emma had two children, Terry and Sylvia, and Emma worked for her brother for a short while. Jim was rich compared to us and had a motorcar; a Vauxhall 10, which he couldn't use until the war ended because he couldn't get any petrol.

CHAPTER TWO

Starting School

I was getting very excited about my fifth birthday as September 1943 approached and I was about to follow my big sister to Tedbury Crescent Infant school *(Now Court Farm Primary School)*. I had been looking forward to this day all through the summer holidays, not knowing what I was really looking forward to. The day finally arrived and I was up early, had a quick wash and brush of my teeth before having my usual bread and jam for breakfast. When I arrived at the school gate and entered the playground I started to feel nervous, as I saw many strangers that I did not know. Mum took me into the classroom, I did not know what to expect, but saw rows and columns of desks, each with seats for two children, one of which was given to me, to be shared with a stranger. Each bench seat had a wooden back rest and a sloping desk top, with two separate flaps to open for books, scarves and gloves and at the top of each desk was a groove for a pen or pencil and at the right hand corner, an ink well. I sat facing the teacher, framed by two large blackboards, there were no toys. The teacher spoke to us all and wrote lessons on the blackboard with chalk, the alphabet, numbers and later spellings, tables or maps and when necessary would explain and teach us all verbally. I can't remember any play learning activities, but I do remember that the toilet blocks were very basic, and were outside in the corner of the playground often with a cold and sometimes rain swept trip to the loo.

I hated my first day at school. I was rather shy and had become accustomed to living in the shadow of my cleverer, older sister and I didn't have any great expectation of success. My problems became worse when I was off school for a long time with whooping cough, which soon afterwards turned to Pneumonia. When I did return to school, I was behind everyone else and never looked forward to going to school. One of the highlights I remember was when an incendiary bomb struck the school. However, my delight was short lived as little damage was inflicted. A series of coughs, colds and sore throats led me to hospital for four days, having my tonsils out. I remember being embarrassed when a nurse put me into the bath with a girl even though I had already had a bath the night before, and then after the operation trying to eat toast that scratched my throat. The combination of tonsils, whooping cough and pneumonia left me with acute breathing problems. My 'get out of school fairy' came to my rescue, sending me for 'Sun Ray' treatment three mornings each week to a treatment centre at Stockland Green, all of this had a devastating effect on my early learning. However, I have to say that I never hurried back to school after any treatment sessions. It came as a harsh shock at the end of a school year, when the teacher read out the class placing and told everyone that I was bottom of the class. In those days there was no sympathetic approach to child psychology, each pupil was top, bottom or somewhere in between. We each had an over all classification and I was bottom. This did nothing for my flagging confidence and didn't make school any more appealing, but at least there was only one way to go from that lowly start. This was in contrast to my sister Connie, three years older, who was always near the top of the class and later passed the 11 plus for Handsworth Grammer School for Girls, while I was pleased when I relinquished the bottom spot to another unfortunate pupil, Dennis Franks.

Great emphasis was placed on accuracy in writing and spelling, and tables every day resembled singing lessons, but the daily repetition brain washed me, and tables were never forgotten. Holidays always came as a welcome break especially Christmas time when, despite the shortages that rationing had brought, coupled with low incomes, lack of refrigeration and orchestrated with the throbbing noise of enemy bombers and the responding volley of gun fire, everyone was determined that Christmas and the festive season would be as special as it could be for us children.

The excitement of Christmas really began to build with a Saturday morning trip to see Santa at Lewiss's in Bull Street, which was in the city centre. Santa Clause could always be found on the top floor of this eight-storey department store, where he would be seated in his Grotto surrounded by Gnomes. The top floor totally gave way to a toy department at Christmas and would be like a Wonderland to small children, who had never had very much. The queue would usually start between the third and fourth floors, winding its way up the staircase to the much longed for gift from Father Christmas, before returning home on the bus, amid excited chatter and joy.

One of my mother's work mates had made a wooden model of a Spitfire and this was a present that was treasured for many years. On Christmas eve the excitement would be building for Santa's arrival, one of Gran's Lisle stockings would be hung at the bottom of the bed, with great hope and expectation that Santa would miraculously avoid both the German bombers and our gunfire, to deliver all of our longed for presents into our stockings; usually a threepenny bit, a shiny new penny, an apple, an orange, a few sweets and possibly a small game, or maybe a ball, all being torn out of the stocking at about four o'clock in the morning. In addition to my prized Spitfire, I also received a second hand Mechano set that had been given away by an older child.

Christmas dinner was also to be special that year as my Dad had obtained a cockerel a couple of months earlier. This prized Christmas dinner had been fattened up with any left over scraps from the table. However, the unfortunate bird that was housed in a homemade pen in our garden, had a vicious streak and gave Gran a nasty peck on her arm when she was feeding it. My Dad, who had never killed anything in his life, had the unenviable task of what can only be described as a fight to the death with this wily old bird, because I can remember fur and feathers flying in all directions before the bird joined the spuds and sprouts on the dinner plates.

Christmas faded into the past with me making things with my Mechano set and Connie learning to knit with a recycled ball of wool. Having started by corking, which entailed the use of a wooden cotton reel with four nails inserted in one end, the wool would be wrapped around the four nails twice, and then by continually lifting the bottom wool over the top one, a woollen corking tube would be made.

When I was seven, I was allowed to walk to and from school, either on my own or with my sister in the mornings, lunch time and evenings. I would turn right at the top of the road, cross over Jerry's Lane by the Leopard Pub, where Gran enjoyed a drink if she had any pension left, and then on into Tedbury Crescent.

Mum told me that the war in North Africa was being won by my Uncle Peter and thousands of other troops, Mum, Dad and Gran would be glued to the wireless every night for the BBC news bulletins, listening and hoping for territorial gains and progress into enemy positions. Our radio ran off a wet and dry accumulator battery that we had to take to the local hardware shop to be recharged. There were still many houses without electricity, which was made worse by the bombing damage that had been targeted at power stations. The heavy loss of ships in the North Atlantic was also adding to food shortages and extending the queues at shops, which tested my Grandmother's cooking skills to the full.

A Sunday treat for my sister and I if Dad was not working, was an adventure by bus to see Granny Grainger and my other aunts and uncles. We would travel by the Number 7 bus, which would take us to Hagley Road where we would then catch the number 2B bus at the Ivy Bush, taking us to Quinton Road. The Golden Hind Pub was the end of our bus journey and we would walk up Quinton Road to number 7, Langford Grove. Chip, a light, fawn coloured, friendly, mongrel dog, would greet us before hugs and kisses from Gran and Granddad and sometimes, aunts and uncles. My

Dad's eldest sister Lucy was already married to Ernest Woodward and my Aunt Phyllis was married to James Constantine who was also in the Army, but in an administration job and although serving abroad, was not fighting the Germans.

My Aunt Phyllis and Aunt Beatrice both worked at the Cadbury Factory at Bournville, which had also turned to the production of machine tools for the war effort. Aunt Florence had joined the Land Army and laboured energetically on a farm, helping to feed the nation at a time when food was very scarce. She told us that this was very hard work, with early morning starts and late finishing times particularly during the summer months at harvest time. My uncles were younger than Dad and next in line was Walter. Walter was a civil servant and considered to be the black sheep of the family, not least for voting Conservative at an early age. Next in line was Peter who was fighting with the Desert Rats and my youngest uncle was Dennis, who had only just left Grammar School.

Monday morning brought me back to school misery again with reading, writing, spelling, arithmetic, and tables where the teachers expected so much of me and I delivered so little. It was a ritual that I had to endure until the next school holidays eventually came round again. Holidays were fun, when I could play, mainly in the road as there were few cars due to the lack of petrol Tip Cat, Hopscotch, Spinning Tops and cricket on the waste ground next to my house. The nearest park was less than a mile away on Court Lane, where all of the steel railings had been removed to be melted down for armament manufacture. The park had swings and roundabouts, a tennis court and a bowling green. A park keeper, usually a retired policeman, would keep a watchful eye over the park and he could hire out tennis and bowling equipment. Coats or jumpers would be spaced apart to act as goalposts. There were proper football pitches but the little delinquents would challenge the park keeper to chase them off from the match pitches, which he was determined to maintain in good condition, until the war was over.

Bad news arrived next door at number 53, when a telegram notifying Mrs. Willets that her husband, a rear gunner on a Lancaster Bomber, had been shot down and was missing, believed killed in action. Other neighbours included Mrs. Pegg who lived opposite, who when she set out for work with her head down and leaning forward so my Granny re-christened her 'here's my head my arse is coming.' Another neighbour a few doors away was openly referred to as the divorcee, divorce was almost unheard of at that time on a council estate. If the same expression were used today, half the road would probably qualify.

I can remember being sent to the greengrocer, a black man who sold fruit and vegetables from his garage in Jerry's Lane, and my Granny would tell me to get spuds or a cabbage from 'the Blackie's' it was so unusual in those days to meet a non-white person, and the days before political correctness had run riotously out of control.

My Mum and Dad were very excited on the 6th June 1944. They said it was D-Day and was a day that had been planned for many months by Winston Churchill and his war cabinet with General Eisenhower the American Chief of Staff. They told me that if the Normandy landings were successful, it would be the beginning of the end of the war. We were fighting back they said, hope and confidence was returning to the Erdington council estate. She also said that The Battle of Britain had been won and more Atlantic convoys were arriving in Liverpool every day, but most of these convoys were bringing vital weapons to back up the invasion, and no improvement would yet be seen in the food arriving at the shops.

Less than a year later on the 8th May 1945 there was more excitement and everyone was cheering. Mum, Dad and all the neighbours were all celebrating VE day, Victory in Europe. Mum said we had beaten the Germans, Germany had unconditionally surrendered, the bombing had stopped and the street parties were being planned. Everyone baked buns, jellies and blancmanges were made, sandwiches of meat paste, (meat was still very scarce), homemade squash, Tizer Pop and pots of tea were all given generously. All sorts of tables and trestles were laid out down the centre of the road to accommodate the excited children and relieved parents. After the street party, bonfires were lit on most street corners. The piano was wheeled out and my Dad played all the popular tunes of the time. 'We'll meet again', 'Pack up your troubles in your old kit bag', 'White cliffs of Dover', 'It's a long way to Tipperary' and many more tunes with people singing and drinking long into the night.

Only three months later, there were more parties as everyone was celebrating the victory over Japan, VJ day, 14th August 1945. Dad explained that war in the Far East had started with a cowardly and unprovoked attack on Pearl Harbour. This was followed by devastatingly cruel battles, waged by a sadistic Imperial Regime, fighting in fierce heat and deplorable conditions through Burma and Singapore. All of this had been brought to a speedy conclusion with atom bombs dropped on Hiroshima and Nagasaki with devastating and lasting effect by nuclear contamination.

We had more parties and no one had any sympathy for the Japanese people, but the legacy left behind by greater nuclear proliferation, combined with the Cold War with Russia, left families with great concern for their future and future generations. The 'H' Bomb, rumoured to be twenty times more powerful than the atom bomb, was a very uncertain influence on our hope for the future, if indeed we had a future. Dad was very worried when Josef Stalin sealed off West Berlin, we would hear daily on the radio about the Berlin Airlift throughout 1948/49 when many flights airlifted food and supplies to West Berlin. The end of the war brought an end to the Coalition Government and in November, the general election brought a staggering result when Winston Churchill, who was the hero and mastermind of the German defeat and being hailed as the saviour of Europe, after standing alone for two years in defiance of the Third Reich, was defeated in the polls, and Clement Atlee and a Labour Government was voted into power.

We would have to wait another seven years before we saw the end of rationing, but a new health service had been introduced, people could look forward again to a more normal way of life. Dad took me to my first football match, a reserve game at St Andrews and I became a life long Birmingham City supporter. We travelled on a number 78 Tram to Aston Cross, where the aroma of HP Sauce and the smell of Malt of Ansell's

Brewery hung like a cloud over most of Aston, before boarding the bus to Small Heath and back to my place of birth. We then walked across a cleared bombsite, where we would pass a hot dog van with a salesman shouting 'with or without onions at no extra charge,' before entering the hallowed ground and the home of city football. Some may have argued that Villa Park was the icon of the city's football, but not me or my Dad.

With the end of the war, I was taken to the seaside for the first time, for seven days' holiday, in a boarding house in Rhyl and I enjoyed my first a ride on a steam train and a donkey ride on the beach. Rationing was still in force and the Utility brand and 'make do and mend' was a stock phrase, whether on holiday or not. Pillboxes and coastal defences were very prominent along all coast lines, reminding us that we had expected to be invaded.

The country was still facing hard times as I travelled to one of the highlights of my week, the Saturday morning matinee at the ABC Plaza cinema Stockland Green. My great favourites were Cowboy Pictures, Roy Rogers and his horse Trigger, Bill Boyd alias Hopalong Cassidy and also comedies such as Laurel and Hardy, Abbot and Costello, Will Hay, and Old mother Riley. I became an ABC minor and as a member of the Saturday club I was able to gain entry for three old pence, a little over one new penny.

These were the pre-television days and we had a great choice of cinemas or picture houses, in addition to the Plaza (now a supermarket) there was the Star Cinema, Slade Road (now a Tyre Workshop) The Mayfair Cinema on College Road (now an Aldi) the Pavilion Cinema at Wylde Green (now Houses and Flats). Erdington Village supported two cinemas The Palace, which is now the Co-op and The Picture House in Erdington, which is now part of Wilton Market; and Sutton Town had two Picture Houses, the Empress and the Odeon, but of all these only the Odeon still survives today.

Food was becoming more plentiful with a greater choice, but fresh fruit such as bananas and oranges were still rarely found in the shops, the egg powder mixed with water was used to make scrambled egg, but was gradually being overtaken by the real thing, eggs in shells produced by chickens. I remember enjoying my first chucky egg with soldiers, a treat that was late arriving on my table, but it can still be argued that we were fed more healthily then than many children are today.

CHAPTER THREE

Secondary School

The winter of 1947 gave me some relief from boring old school, when the worst snow conditions ever recorded hit the Midlands, causing our school to close for a long period, with snowdrifts over three feet deep and prolonged freezing temperatures preventing a thaw for weeks. Making snowmen, sliding and sledging were much better than a claustrophobic classroom. But eventually the thaw came with the snow giving way to grey slush and there were only a few more weeks of lessons before another summer holiday arrived.

I was taken on a second holiday together with Granny to Margate travelling by charabanc. We stopped in a boarding house within walking distance from the sea. The whole family enjoyed the sea and sunshine and we had a great time with buckets and spades on the beach with the aroma of seaweed and the smell of cockles, mussels and whelks and we were all mesmerised by the antics of Punch and Judy with Gran having the occasional glass of stout, while my Dad tried to find a drink as good as his much prized Ansell's Mild, all making its contribution to a memorable change from school work, and the industrial atmosphere of city life.

Secondary School was beckoning as September arrived and as my health improved, so did my school work as my mother had a blind determination that I should follow my sister to Grammar School. Needless to say, I sat the exam twice and failed twice. She then tried to get me into a school in Boldmere, but I was just as determined to go with my mates, walking mornings, lunch times and evenings, a little over a mile down Witton Lodge Road to Hastings Road Secondary Modern School. I was still having jam sandwiches for breakfast, if I had preferred marmalade they could have called me Paddington Bear. Although a particular treat on Monday morning, if we had had a bit of beef for Sunday lunch, was dripping toast with the fat and jelly left over from the roast.

I eagerly looked forward to my tenth birthday. It was to be my first birthday party with school friends invited jellies, cakes and all manner of goodies that had been so scarce thoughout the whole of the war years. My prized birthday present was a mouth organ, which gave me an ambition to follow my father's musical ability and within a few days I had mastered 'London Bridge is falling down' and a few other tunes. My proud mother was so impressed that she encouraged me by buying a second-hand 12 bass piano accordion for my eleventh birthday, which led to music lessons and eventually rising to the dizzy heights of starring at a Stockland Green youth concert.

My father's determination to provide for his growing family had driven him to find a second job, working evenings and weekends doing bar work at the Boldmere Pub (now the Harvester), whilst this helped the family budget, it also helped support his high consumption of cigarettes. My Grandmother would, with the aid of a walking stick as arthritis was now having a crippling effect on her mobility, meet her friends in the Leopard Pub and my Dad's sister, Floss, had returned home from working on the land to look after her ageing parents Granny Grainger was now diabetic and in poor health.

The family's weekly treat at this time occurred on Sunday evening, when my mother would take my sister and me to the Pavilion Cinema, Wylde Green, catching a number 28 bus, which would drop us outside the cinema. We would go every Sunday regardless of what films were being shown. The highlight at the interval, in addition to ice cream, was the organ, which would appear out of the floor in front of the stage and would entertain the audience, before the feature film was shown. My Dad didn't come with us as he would be pulling pints in the pub.

Christmas time was always a great reunion for the Grainger family in that, on Boxing Day, almost all of the aunts, uncles and cousins converged on Langford Grove. This was one of the rare opportunities that I would get to meet my Grainger cousins. Presents would be exchanged and Aunt Floss would organise games and keep all of the kids occupied, while the grown ups argued about politics and the merits of Aston Villa and Birmingham City. Granny Grainger cooked apple and fruit pies with produce from the garden that had been preserved from the summer months and the remains of a huge turkey were devoured amid much laughter and merriment.

By the age of ten, my sister and I would be expected to do the weekly shopping, a list would have been carefully written out by Mum and we would walk to the

Co-op at Perry Common circle. The shop was fully staffed, as in those days there was no self-service; customers would be served with their requirements and the money would be handed over together with their Co-op number, 171852, which would accrue into a dividend dependent on how much was spent. The money and the number were placed in a metal overhead container, which would fly across on wires to the cashier who was centrally situated. The cashier would then check the bill, calculate the change and together with a copy of the dividend receipt send the container flying back across the wires to the assistant, who would return it to the customer. We would then walk back home sharing the heavy bags, complete with the weekly shopping, change and dividend receipt.

Both of my parents were Christians and any form or document that had to be filled in, the Religion notated was C of E, although neither of them went to church, except for weddings, funerals and baptisms. Both my sister and I had been christened and by now were expected to attend Sunday school. I thought, 'as if going to school five days in the week wasn't enough.' My first introduction to religion was by being dragged along by my sister to St Margaret's C of E Church at Somerset Road off Court Lane, which I thought was even more boring than day school. Although joining the scouts did offer some relief, until the scoutmaster was allegedly arrested on suspicion of child abuse. My sister decided that the Congregational Church would be more uplifting for her and I, but it was short lived, as there was no Youth Club or Scout Pack, so my next religious encounter was to be the Methodist Church at Stockland Green. It must be said that Connie could have been pursuing prospective boyfriends at this time. However, it did have a good youth club, plus Boy Scout and Girl Guide Packs. I moved up from the Cubs to the Scouts and eventually became a Patrol Leader with badges all up my arm; at this stage I was still more practical than academic.

When I returned from my first Scout camp, I learned that my Granny Grainger had died, but I do not remember much sense of grief as visits to see her were infrequent. I enjoyed my scouting days, but never really found camping that exciting. My aversion of the great outdoors with the lack of home comforts was later endorsed with a caravan holiday, one cold bleak Easter break from school, at my Aunt Emma's caravan, when the frost by night made it possible for me to scrape ice off the inside of the windows first thing in the morning. The wind-driven drizzly rain by day kept me in doors in a confined space for most of the short and memorable holiday for all of the wrong reasons. The only bright spot was the all day Monopoly games, which may have given me some ideas about my future, although it was not uncommon when someone lost prematurely, for the houses and hotels in Mayfair and Park Lane, to be sent flying in all directions.

My progress at Hastings Road Secondary School was much improved, possibly because all of the high flyers had gone to Grammar School and Perry Common pupils were not that bright. My mother was again determined that I should have the best possible education and arranged for me to sit the entry exam for the Technical School, which to everyone's amazement, including my own, I passed at the second attempt. Eureka! I had finally passed something. It has to be said that my mother, who always empathised with the underdog, worked very hard with me and gave me every possible encouragement to build my self-confidence.

By the time I had reached my thirteenth birthday Mum's efforts were rewarded and together with playing my accordion party pieces for unsuspecting visitors who had not had the foresight to have a pre planned escape route, coupled with their encouraging applause, helped me to become a much more self assured teenager. I went from strength to strength at Handsworth Technical School, enjoying the practical subjects of technical drawing, and metalwork. I particularly remember trying to wipe a lead joint unsuccessfully, which finished as a lump of molten metal on the bench. I am very thankful for my mother's determination, as the Technical School was to shape my future career and also make a useful personal contribution later in life.

It was while I was laying bricks one afternoon that the teacher sombrely informed the class that King George the sixth had died earlier that day, 6th February 1952. This was unexpected news and meant that our next monarch would be a queen.

The brick laying and other practical training that I was receiving was to make a big contribution in later life. I also received a maximum mark for a 25 page history project on architecture and achieved third place in the year's overall assessment. This was a mighty climb from being bottom of the class of 35 pupils in the early days.

The following year brought the Coronation of Queen Elizabeth II and 2nd June 1953 was declared a national holiday and more street parties were organised, but I had the opportunity to go shooting with my Uncle Jim and

Cousin Ray at Grindleford in the Derbyshire Dales and the rabbits were a much bigger attraction than a bun fight in the street. Mount Everest had been conquered for the first time a few days before by Sir Edmund Hillary and Sherpa Tensing, but the news did not filter through until the day after the Coronation.

After my first year at the Tech, I was devastated when my Granny Bowdler died suddenly with a brain haemorrhage. My Grandmother had always lived with us and had mothered me through the war years. She had always been there with a plaster for scuffed knees and encouragement through my unhappy early school years and when things went wrong, she was my special Granny.

During the summer school holiday swimming became the rage with my friends and neighbours, Kenny and Dennis Roadnight and Kenny Pegg. We would go swimming nearly everyday to Kingstanding Swimming Baths. I became a strong swimmer and enjoyed diving from the boards, racing and somersaulting into the pool, until some other craze took its place. On rainy days card games such as snap, gin rummy and sevens would pass a few hours away.

Although I was doing much better at school, this did not qualify me to stay on to take 'O' Level examinations and I left school after my fifteenth birthday with great joy that a life sentence had finally come to an end. Connie had left school two years earlier at the age of sixteen after sitting her 'O' level exams. She went on to secretarial training at ICI Witton and later became a legal secretary.

Mum, the go-getter, had saved for and bought an Insurance Book and was now working as a

Commissioned Agent selling insurance policies and collecting premiums for The Royal Liver Friendly Society. She would cycle to the various rounds through all weathers, which spread from Aston to Four Oaks and Streetly, doing different rounds on different days each week. This gave her a great deal of flexibility to keep her eye on two teenage children. My Dad had also found better-paid employment as a brass finisher and although he was offered a foreman's job he declined it as he did not want the extra responsibility.

I had been inspired by my Dad's earlier trips to St Andrews and I was now a regular Birmingham City supporter. They were in the first division, the top league at that time and I supported them at their first game under floodlights when they played against Dynamo Zagreb, in the Inter City Fairs cup and drawing 3-3, they later went on to draw 4 -4 with Barcelona and lost 2-1 in the replay. I can also vividly remember Birmingham knocking Manchester United out of the FA.Cup with a 1-0 victory, scoring in the first minute of the game.

I was very keen on all sport, especially football and cricket. Dad had regularly taken me to watch Aston Unity a top Birmingham League team whose ground was then in Court Lane, almost next to the Greyhound Pub. Several retired Warwickshire players including Eric Hollies and past England players could often be seen in this league on Saturday afternoons.

Cycling was to be the next craze and having sold my prized accordion, much to the relief of the visitors I bought a brand new Dawes racing bike and with my school friend, Raymond Garret, we cycled most weekends, the longest journey being to visit Raymond's Grandmother in Swindon.

I had also applied for a Saturday job at Jackson's the Tailors, on the corner of Pope Street and New Street, Birmingham. They gave me the job and paid me fifteen shillings (75p) a day, a shilling for every year of my age, for working from 10 o'clock until 5.30. I either helped to take down measurements shouted out by the tailor as he measured the customer, or wrapped up suits that were being collected and generally helped to keep the shop tidy, when all manner of rolls of material had been reeled out to induce a sale. Out of my 75p I would go to Woolworth's for dinner, dining out was a novelty, I always had sausages and mash 1s 8d (just over 8p) and I also had to pay my own bus fare both ways. Woolworths was situated almost opposite the Theatre Royal, New Street, where my Mum had taken me to Pantomimes when I was younger. When I was about to leave school I was offered a full time job in retail with Jackson's, leading to management training, but I was more interested in engineering and declined the offer.

Chapter Four

Finding a Job

In my last few weeks at school, it was announced to the class that there was a job opportunity at a firm of central heating engineers, in Rea Street, Digbeth. The year was 1952 and with very few houses centrally heated, I reckoned that heating was something for the future and could provide good career prospects. So with Mum, I arranged an interview and being the only candidate, I got the job. My ability to succeed when I was the only competitor was unbounded. I would serve a five year apprenticeship and would start as a tracer, having done technical drawing at school. The starting wage was £1 and 7shillings per week and at the end of the apprenticeship, I was guaranteed to earn at least £10 per week. This appealed to me as a huge sum of money at the time. Two weeks after leaving school, I started work, catching two buses to Seymour Sweet & Co, Heating Engineers.

My first day was spent making a traced copy with a pencil on a huge sheet of tracing paper of an architectural drawing, this was checked and I was shown the importance of accuracy and neatness. When my a tracing with pencil was considered good enough, I was shown how to trace using an ink drawing pen on tracing paper this was much more exacting, as ink smudged easily and was more difficult to rectify. Having mastered this, I went onto tracing on canvas sheet, which was even more difficult to correct any mistakes. In fact I had done so much tracing that my friends could have called me Tracey. I also had to learn to do small printed block capitals in ink, very neatly, in order to add notes to drawings.

The lighter side of Seymour Sweet & Co. was that they had their own cricket team and were looking for potential players. After purchasing whites out of my meagre income, I joined the cricket team, playing Village Green cricket at places like Middleton, Hammerwich, St. Margaret's Hospital and the like. In the football season I played for Four Oaks Boys Club in the Sutton Youth League, and I also played cricket for them in the summer months.

I was only just sixteen when I had to attend my first site meeting on my own; the site was at Kings Norton Comprehensive School, a project that was under construction at that time. I was told that no one else was available and I would provide a presence and take notes. I travelled by bus and arrived late and found my way to a wooden hut, heaving with architects, surveyors, engineers and contractors, who could not resist the temptation to make life uncomfortable, for what they saw was an inexperienced spotty faced little upstart. However, it was all part of my learning curve. My drawing skills were improving as I was now expected to produce simple scale drawings for brackets and oil tanks etc. I also had to attend college one day each week to study for my National Certificate of Education. I made a great effort, working hard for this three year course. If I could complete the course successfully in the three years, without any re-takes, it would qualify me for the National College for Heating, Ventilation and Air Conditioning Engineers in London.

After working and saving for nine months, I planned a holiday with military precision in conjunction with my cycling friend, Raymond Garret, to cycle to the Lake District. All Youth Hostels were pre-booked together with packed lunches. Our plan was to tour as many lakes as possible and to attempt a mighty climb, cycling up the Kirkstone Pass, near Ambleside and then continue the tour of Windermere, Coniston and Buttermere. This was my first introduction to the land of Wordsworth and Potter, but the awe inspiring beauty of the panoramic scenery, which had provided their literary inspiration, was to the sow the seeds for my return many times years later. With the summer break from work coming to an end, the return journey was much quicker, as spending two weeks in the saddle we were by now both racing fit. It has to be said that most of the military planning had been done for Mum's sake, as at sixteen, she still was very protective of not so little me.

On returning to work I was given more complicated drawing work. Ken Jones, a senior engineer, taught me how to calculate heat losses and radiator sizing and I was gradually becoming a proficient draughtsman. My college work was on schedule, passing the first year maths, physics, English and engineering drawing, with maths being my strongest subject. I was studying at Aston Technical College, which later became Aston University.

Driving lessons were by now very high on my list of priorities. I applied for my provisional licence to arrive on my sixteenth birthday, but sadly a few days later I broke my wrist playing football and driving was off the agenda for six weeks. My parents had started driving lessons with the British School of Motoring and had purchased a very old Austin Litchfield car, which had been well cared for by all of its many previous owners. Street credibility was not an issue in those days, to have any sort of a car on a council estate elevated the family to snob status.

My mother was very slow to learn to drive, which was particularly sad, as she was still cycling every day, covering a large area with her work. As soon as I was able, I asked a friend at work to give me some lessons in the lunch hour in his Austin Seven, a car which had not been manufactured since 1939, but in spite of this, it was still a great help, as every time I stalled the engine, I had to get out, to wind it up by hand to get it re started and changing gear necessitated double de clutching. It has to be said that Mum was driving her husband into something that was definitely not his forte, however he took his test on a January morning and failed first time. I took my test in more favourable weather conditions and with extra practice with work mates, passed first time. To my delight, I became the family chauffeur, even after my father had passed the test at the second attempt, as he was never keen on driving and Stirling Moss was never in any danger of competition from Dad.

Mum was determined to have space to garage the prized Austin Litchfield. I should mention that this car had huge headlights, running boards and indicators, which mechanically came out of each side of the car, when so directed. The search was underway for another council house, which was found in the same road number 143. This house had space for off street parking and had a ramshackle, rusting galvanised garage at the rear and was to be our next home, and the move from number 51 to 143 was completed.

My work was progressing well and I was enjoying the work, doing detailed boiler house drawings in ink on canvas as well as taking off quantities and estimating costs, in order to submit tenders for projects around the Midlands. The company was split into two; half of the work was for the Coal Board and involved all mechanical services for Pithead Baths and offices, mainly using steam from other operations in the Colliery. The work was quite widespread with projects for South Wales, Lancashire and Yorkshire Coal Boards. Surveys usually involved an over night stay in a cheap hotel. Mr. Gill, the Managing Director, not only looked like scrooge, but this Judea Yorkshire cross, had deep pockets and short arms where money was concerned. My first trip to a coalmine was to a Yorkshire pit, travelling with the labour supervisor, Frank Wakefield, in his Ford Popular which was company owned and I was treated on expenses to my first Chinese meal, a greasy Chow Mein followed by a trip to the cinema showing Rock Around the Clock with Bill Haley and the Comets.

The other half of the company dealt with all other work, schools, hospitals, factories and offices; indeed any project that required heating or ventilation. This was headed by Ron Skinner, also a keen cricketer and was a pleasure to work for. As an apprentice I would get experience on either team depending on which was the busiest.

My apprenticeship was advancing and I was working very hard in the final year of my National Certificate.

I had been deferred from doing my National Service, which was still compulsory. If I passed the final year, I knew that within a few months I would be off to the Borough Polytechnic in London, now London South Bank University, for a full time course. I was now designing, calculating, estimating, surveying, drawing and managing all manner of heating projects.

Connie had auditioned for Highbury Little Theatre and all her spare time was taken up with rehearsing, acting and any other job that needed doing, while she was now working as a legal secretary for solicitors' Davies, Arnold & Barrett in Cherry Street, Birmingham.

A number of very significant political changes were taking place at this time and Winston Churchill had been re-elected in 1951 after a fairly dismal period under the Atlee Government, which had seen an era of nationalisation, in particular the railways and the mining industries, which led to power cuts and a three day working week. Churchill stepped down in 1955, making way for Anthony Eden who took the country back to war in 1956 as a result of the Suez crisis and although the war only lasted two weeks it had a lasting effect on the supply of oil from the Middle East. Petrol rationing came in as well as a change in regulations, which permitted my Mum to drive unaccompanied on a provisional licence and finally, at long last, led to her passing her driving test after three years of perseverance. The Austin Lichfield was sold to a vintage collector and a nearly-new cream Austin A30 was purchased.

There was one further highlight for me, as 1956 was the year Birmingham City reached the FA Cup Final and although this had happened once before, it was long before I had been born. Sadly it ended in disappointment, when they were beaten 3-1 by Manchester City in the final.

I passed my third and final year exams and gained my first qualification, a National Certificate in Mechanical Engineering and as a result one Sunday afternoon in early September 1957, I nervously travelled to a college hostel in Sydenham Hill near Crystal Palace, leaving home for the first time. I shared a room with five other guys all doing the same course and had arrived from various other heating consultants and contractors throughout the country. The hostel was fairly basic, but did have a table tennis facility, a television lounge and a large room for studying. Social functions were arranged with nearby teacher training colleges, usually Philippa Fawcett College in Streatham. The course at the National College for Heating, Ventilation and Air Conditioning Engineers was attached to the Borough Polytechnic on the South Bank.

The course was only one-year duration, but was very concentrated with many subjects being studied; advanced maths, heating, ventilation, air conditioning, mechanics of fluids, fan engineering and heat transfer. Studying left little time for the social life seen in University today. However, I did play football at Catford on Saturday afternoons and sometimes rugby for the college, if I was free and they were desperate, followed by the odd pint with John Davies, a keen rugby player from Nottingham.

I travelled to college each day by train from Sydenham Hill station to the Elephant and Castle via Brixton and then on by foot to tutorials at the Borough Poly. After returning back to the Hostel on the 6th of February 1958 I was enjoying my evening meal, when the news filtered through that the plane carrying Manchester United's Busby Babes back from Munich had crashed on take off, in freezing foggy conditions, with the loss of most of the team. This was so unbelievable at the time, that I thought it was a joke in bad taste, but on listening to the news the next morning the full extent of the horror became apparent, with the loss of young international stars, Tommy Taylor and Duncan Edwards, together with the loss and injury of many other football legends.

The year passed very quickly and I returned back home to my family and back to work. All of the sport resumed and a work friend Billy Drew was about to follow my footsteps to college in London.

The year at college had given me more confidence than was good for me, because less than a year after I returned to work, I had a disagreement with the boss, the dreaded scrooge, Mr. Gill, and after laughing at some of my bosses proposals on a particular design, I got the sack and quickly learned that to laugh at someone, at the height of a disagreement, really winds them up. No written warnings in those days. It was pack your bags, a week's pay of £7 in lieu of notice, and goodbye Mr. Chips. I hadn't even reached the promised £10 a week.

Mr. Gill was a diminutive Yorkshire man, always wore a suit, waistcoat and tie and facially had St. Bernard dog features, with puffy jowls and badly fitting false teeth; his other drawback was that he was almost totally deaf without his hearing aid. He used the hearing aid to good effect, switching it off if he did not want to hear what was being said to him. This was particularly annoying if anyone asked for a pay rise, which to a Yorkshire man was like asking him to donate an organ, he would reach into his waistcoat pocket and a distinct click could be heard, as the hearing aid was switched off. Try to explain why you deserve a pay rise to someone that can't hear.

I should say that at this stage I was probably better qualified than Mr. Gill and had been taught the latest methods and technology, which could have saved time and money for the company. Mr. Gill was not convinced and I quickly learned that discretion in the future would be the better part of valour. I was miffed by my current predicament, as I had just started going out with my first ever girlfriend Barbara, from the typing pool, although she fancied me something rotten, she did not leave much of an impression, as I can't remember her surname. She did, to her credit, have an Austin Healy Sprite, which was very impressive to travel around in, but definitely not a courting car.

Signing on at the labour exchange every two weeks was a new and humbling experience, but it probably accelerated my call up for National Service, so that I could be removed from the unemployment figures and that was the end of the short romance.

CHAPTER FIVE

National Service

I was still keeping in touch with my old work mates while seeking alternative employment, Bill Drew and Jim Kelly were good friends and fellow cricketers. Bill was later to make a significant contribution to my life. He was still at college, while I was trying to find gainful employment, which was very elusive, when all employers would know that it could be a matter of weeks before I was called for National Service.

The notification arrived on the 1st. November 1959; an official looking buff coloured envelope enclosing a letter from the War Office advised me that Her Majesty the Queen required my services in the Royal Air Force. I had to report to RAF Cardington on 26th November and a travel warrant was enclosed for the train from New Street Station to Cardington in Bedfordshire.

As I was entering the train I met up with another victim and old school friend, Bob Golden, which provided a little comfort as we both waved goodbye to our families on the station, travelling to a new, spartan and regimented environment.

An air force blue RAF covered lorry met us at Cardington Station and provided an uncomfortable ride to the barracks. We were to be housed in a wooden hut, which was to be a shared home with thirty other recruits. We were at Cardington for about ten days having extensive medical checks, drop them and cough, aptitude tests, and relatively light training, before being kitted out with kit bag, two uniforms (one dress, the other working), regulation underwear, boots, beret, cap, Nursemaid, (this was not what you may think), it was a sewing and darning kit, in addition to the proverbial mug and cutlery. I was now pronounced fit and ready to serve my Queen and country.

Attending my first Pay Parade, 5074171 aircraftsman Grainger, marched up to the paymasters table, saluted and received £1 - 7shillings which by coincidence equalled my first pay packet as an apprentice. From my weekly fortune, I had to buy cleaning materials and other sundries in addition to having a good time. As George Best once said when asked what he had done with all of his money, he hinted that it was spent on gorgeous women, wild parties and booze and the rest he just squandered. I was left with £1 a week to squander on cigarettes and other luxuries.

Being the end of November and the beginning of an early severe winter, scavenging for fuel to stoke the stove in the centre of the hut was a high priority for the thirty potential airmen that lived there. I can confirm that we had little success and everyone had to keep moving to keep warm.

The order was posted on the hut notice board that everyone had to be packed and ready for transportation to the station after breakfast next morning. Bob and I, together with all of the recruits were heading for RAF Bridgnorth, for eight weeks' basic training. We were allocated the same billet and the same flight. A flight was forty strong and was divided into two billets with twenty airmen in each. A drill corporal had his own room at the end of each billet all housed in wooden huts, with a stove in the centre. The floors were highly polished, which had to be maintained to a high gloss, to the extent that everyone slid around the floor on pads, to minimise the manual daily polishing with bumpers.

It was the drill corporal's job to look like a member of the Gestapo, instil fear like the Gestapo, and in eight weeks transform forty fairly soft, unfit specimens into a disciplined military unit.

November was very cold that year but from six o'clock in the morning until nine o'clock at night everything was done at double time, no one was allowed to walk, we had to run everywhere. Each day consisted of drill, P.E., kit inspections, spud bashing or other domestic duties, some relief came in the lecture room, when we were taught how to salute properly, when to salute and who to salute, and we were trained in hygiene and cleanliness, as it was an offence to be sick. I learned all of the ranks in all three services, as they all had to be saluted, in addition the history and traditions of the Royal Air Force, all of which was drilled into each airman with pride.

Most of the newly established airmen in my billet had all been deferred and were generally well qualified an architect, a quantity surveyor and a policeman to name but a few. In addition, there were some guys who had joined as regular airmen and signed up for a number of years as a career move. One recruit in a bed near to me had signed up for nine years, after completing a degree in modern languages to become an RAF interpreter in

Russian. All had to complete basic training and to pass out. If an airman failed any of the tests or discipline, the poor sod could be put back two weeks to the next flight ad infinitum. Something to be avoided at all costs, as the desire to escape this austere regime was compelling.

Sunday was a day of rest, but for any airmen confined to camp, it was compulsory to attend Church Parade in Dress uniform, where we were divided by denomination, C of E, RC or OD (Other Denominations). My earlier nomadic church attendance left me with a dilemma, but I chose the ODs as it covered a multitude of sinners.

Three weeks into training brought some relief as the drill instructors stated that they were in need of a break from this miserable shower of no hope airmen for Christmas. As a result seven days' leave was granted. A week at home for Christmas in a warm house being pampered by mother, I thought I had died and gone to Heaven.

A week later, a return to hell, though in fairness having been away from home for a year at college, I didn't find it as difficult and humiliating as some of my compatriots. I was quite fit from all the sport I played and I accepted that the training had a purpose, even if some of the training was a bit over the top. Being sent into a room filled with tear gas with a gas mask on and being asked to remove it to see the difference was one that springs to mind.

Basic training in fire fighting and the uses of the various extinguishers I could accept more easily. I enjoyed the firing range and shooting with a Bren gun with live ammunition and found it quite stimulating and I was quite a good shot, maybe my earlier practice shooting rabbits with my uncle had helped. I was awarded my marksman's badge, which I proudly sewed on to the right sleeve of my jacket; the Nursemaid Kit had come in use after all.

After returning from the Christmas break, a route march was planned for the first week in January. The morning of the planned route march I awoke early to find deep snow had fallen over night, surely the march would be postponed, only to be told that endurance and navigational skills would be enhanced by the difficult conditions.

The D.I. barked, 'Wars aren't only fought in the summer Laddy'. Our billet was split into groups of six, with each group being given a packed lunch, a map, a compass and a grid reference to be reached by midday and once there we were to return to camp by the same route.

The architect from the Mumbles in South Wales took charge, saying he knew all about grid references and map reading so we all followed this disorientated Welshman with blind faith, tramping through deep snow in the Wyre Forest following the river Severn, which by midday and in deep snow, was a long way from Bridgnorth. We stopped somewhere in the middle of the Wyre Forest, exhausted and in need of sustenance only to be told by the Welshman, that we were only half way to the map reference that we had been given. He admitted that there must be something wrong with the map reference that he was working to, or more likely he had cocked it up. People close to me would know of my phobia of the Welsh and this guy was doing nothing to change that point of view. However, we eventually arrived in Bewdley, telephoned the camp, caught a bus, and arrived back at camp at around six o'clock in the evening feeling very wet cold and tired. Looking on the bright side as I always did, I said, 'It was a day out after all'.

I'm on the extreme left end of the middle row, Bob Golden extreme left back row, and the Welsh (Twit) map reading 'expert' is last on right on back row.

More training, drill instruction, kit inspections, aptitude tests, medicals, inoculations and eventually career interviews followed, which gave the RAF the opportunity to induce National Service recruits to sign on, to make the RAF a career. More pay and a career of your choice were the incentives. I was not convinced, but I still had to select some of the jobs on offer. My first choice was meteorology, the second choice was instrument engineer and thirdly air frame engineering.

I was not at all surprised when I was told that none of these would be available, unless I signed on for a minimum of five years. A proposal that I did not find very appealing and I went on to pass a Morse test, and be trained as a wireless operator. The Morse test entailed identifying same or different paired patterns of dots and dashes.

The Pass Out Parade was rapidly approaching, our drill was now at a very high standard, forty airmen were able to simultaneously fix bayonets with one click, present arms, shoulder arms, about turn, all with great precision. We invited our families. Our uniforms were all smartly pressed, brass buttons shining in the sunshine. Boots polished and honed to a high gloss. The drill display was inspired by the strains of the Air Force March and the Dam Busters being played by the RAF Band, this was an occasion of achievement and pride. It was a particularly proud day for relatives watching, but even for this National Serviceman I, who had been torn from my chosen career, was very proud to be in the RAF and British that day.

Before leaving Bridgnorth for two weeks' leave, I collected my mobilisation and travel warrants, with orders for me to report to number 3 Signals School RAF Compton Basset in Wiltshire for signals training. I said goodbye to all of the individuals who had become a team in eight tempestuous weeks including Bob Golden who had signed up for three years, so he was to be trained elsewhere. However, we did keep in touch and later Bob asked me to be his best man, when he was married in uniform at St. Barnabas Church on Erdington High Street.

I arrived at RAF Compton Bassett on a spring Sunday afternoon, only to find that the accommodation was much the same as Bridgnorth, but a much more civilised regime was awaiting me for the next twenty weeks, eighteen of which I would be learning to send and receive Morse code, together with other signals procedures.

After an early breakfast on Monday morning all documentation was checked and I had to swear and sign the Official Secrets Act. My signals course would not be starting for two weeks and in the meantime I was assigned to painting the pipes in the boiler house. As I was whiling away my time painting, it reminded me of all of the drawings of pipes that I had done before entering the RAF. This enhancement of war office property must have been a regular stop gap, because the pipes had so many coats of paint, they did not require lagging. However there was much more freedom of movement when not pipe painting and there were no problems in visiting the local hostelry in civilian clothes, the White Horse Pub, which was the nearest watering hole to the camp.

The two weeks passed slowly, but new friends were made and eventually the eighteen-week course started. After eighteen week's training we would expect to send and receive Morse code at eighteen five-letter words per minute and have learned many shortened Q codes used by pilot signallers. The training system was a simple form of brain washing. Four characters of the alphabet were selected and each letter was transmitted in its Morse format to the trainee through earphones. Each character was repeated three times and every character had to be written down as it was received. As the week progressed each character was only sent randomly once.

The second week, four new characters were added and at the end of the week, trainees were tested randomly on all eight characters.

This progressed weekly until all 26 letters and 10 numerical digits were known at an approximate speed of eight words per minute. This had taken nine weeks, half of the course. From then on the speed was increased by two words per minute each week with weekly tests for accuracy. This continued until the whole group of twenty signallers could send and receive Morse code accurately at eighteen words per minute. At night I could hear dots and dashes in my sleep.

On passing the course I was awarded a Sparks Badge, my rank rose to LAC (Leading Air Craftsman) with an increase in pay to 30 shillings (£1.50) per week, which was hardly likely to bring the British economy to its knees.

Thirty six hour passes could be obtained most weekends with coaches leaving the camp at lunchtime Saturday and returning from Cambridge Street, Birmingham at 23.00 Sunday night, but as the coaches also dropped off air personnel at RAF Lyneham and Yatesbury, it would often be 3.00am before my return to bed, a lot of trouble and ill afforded expense for less than 36 hours at home. However for Mum's sake, I did make the journey home once a month.

After completion of the course, most of the crew that I had trained with were all ordered to report to 399 Signals unit, RAF Digby, in Lincolnshire for advanced wireless operator training. We were again issued with travel warrants and documentation and given seven days' leave, a week which passed quickly, but it was nice to be home to share the experiences with my family.

RAF Digby was a top secret signals establishment, ID had to be carried at all times and the security to get in and out of the Radio School was via two steel gates. After getting through the first one, it was closed and ID checked, before the second gate was opened and entry into the wireless school was possible. I have to mention that this was also a training camp for aerial riggers and there must have been at least twenty 360 feet high transmitter masts, which I thought was a bit of a giveaway that it was a signals establishment.

The accommodation was very comfortable with centrally heated rooms and the best food that I experienced throughout the whole of my National Service, but RAF Digby was very isolated and apart from country walks, and the NAAFI, there was very little to do.

I made friends with a guy named Peter Walsh, who was a very devout Presbyterian and I attended church services with Peter most Sundays. This added another denomination to the list of churches I had already attended. I quickly realised that I knew no bounds where ecumenicalism was concerned.

The twelve-week course consisted of leaning additional Morse characters to cover languages other than English and to increase the speed from 18 to 26 words per minute. I also had to learn the formats for passing on coded messages to code breakers and interpreters. Some basic direction finding techniques were also learned. RAF Digby is still operational today, but little information will be found about 399 Signals unit, as this information is still restricted, even up to the present time.

Getting home was particularly difficult even though forty-eight hour passes were readily available. Out of desperation to get away from this isolated camp,

I accepted a lift as a pillion passenger on a motorbike to Nuneaton with the return from Nuneaton on Sunday night. This appeared to be quite good as it was a simple journey home to and from Nuneaton. The vital point that I had overlooked was that I had no leathers and no amount of jumpers and overcoats could have prepared me for the return journey. Within a short distance I was worrying about hypothermia; my knees were frozen solid to the extent that I could not straighten them to get off the bike. It did not take long for me to decline the offer of a pillion ride the next time the opportunity came along.

There was great speculation about the next posting, as half of my National Service had now been taken up in training, surely the training must come to an end sometime. I learned that my next destination was to be number 5 Signals wing RAF Butzweilerhof in Germany. The orders came that I was to get two weeks' mobilisation leave and would then be flown from RAF Manston in Kent, to RAF Wildenrath in Germany and then by road to RAF Butzweilerhof, which was situated just North of Cologne (Köln).

RAF Butzweilerhof was a large base, which supported its own cinema and swimming pool with all other sporting facilities. In addition to the signals wing it also accommodated 420 Recovery and Salvage Squadron, which was a large motor vehicle maintenance unit. The accommodation was comfortable and centrally heated, with four and six bedded rooms.

The signals unit was divided into four watches and would have four duty cycles, which accommodated 24 hour coverage of radio signals 365 days a year. On each watch, 30 highly trained radio operators would man 60 high-powered radio receivers. The work that I was doing was and still is classified and cannot be described further.

The one draw back about this system was that it was necessary to work from midnight to 8am every forth night. The good thing was that everyone only worked two days in every four. So effectively by taking two working days' leave, I could have six clear days to travel if I left straight after night shift and did not return until my 8am duty, on the seventh day.

Pay was still were meagre, about two Deutschmarks a week, but the bus fare into Cologne was only three pfennigs (100 to the Mark), 200 free cigarettes each week by coupon, Whiskey or Rum was the equivalent of 4d per shot and we were awarded free rail travel up to 50 miles beyond the German Border, which gave me ample opportunity to travel at low cost.

The combination of the six day breaks and 50mile travel warrants enabled me to have: a long weekend in Winterberg skiing, which was situated about two hours by coach from Cologne and was my first attempt at skiing on real snow so I had many falls, to everyone's delight; a long weekend in Amsterdam; a seven-day holiday in Copenhagen; seven days' holiday in Venice; plus, one trip home, all this in the eleven months that I was stationed in Germany, which was more than I had ever travelled in my life.

The summer was hot and the swimming pool was much appreciated during off duty periods and the NAAFI club supported many demob parties, this together with the cinema provided light entertainment at little cost. Butzweilerhof also supported its own football league and I played for the combined C-D watch team, playing some of the best footy in my life probably, because it was the only time I was really in peak condition. Playing centre forward I scored a hat trick in a 3-3 draw against the Sergeant's Mess team. Not quite the Bundesliga, but it gave me much pleasure.

Sightseeing in Cologne was only a bus ride away, where the main centre of attraction in Cologne was the Dom Cathedral and high up in one of the spires were slide pictures showing the total destruction of Cologne by British bombers up until 1945. The Cathedral was never hit and by the time I arrived there in 1960 the city had been totally rebuilt and had a very modern road layout with a good and efficient transport system.

The major festival of the year other than Christmas was Rosenmontag, a carnival enjoyed by most German speaking countries including Austria and Switzerland. The literal translation is Rose Monday, but for some unknown reason is always celebrated on a Tuesday and it is a national holiday. The 'Karneval' is a continuation of the old traditions of being slaves and masters for a day and the Mardi Gras procession consists of many floats with people dressed in traditional costumes throwing sweets to the children, with dancing and heavy drinking in the streets. This was a great day to be off duty to enjoy the celebrations.

Christmas day 1960 was a sleep day after being on duty from midnight to 8am, but after only a short sleep I arose to be served Christmas dinner cooked by intoxicated chefs and served by the officers as tradition dictated. New Year's Eve duty rota also worked out reasonably well, as I was off duty and travelled into Cologne to see in the New Year in German style, drinking into the early hours of the morning, before reporting for duty at 8am nursing an almighty hangover.

RAF Butzweilerhof was originally Cologne's main airport and was taken over by the RAF in 1951 and closed down at the beginning of 1967. The original terminal building and control tower are listed buildings, but in 2007 most of the other buildings were being demolished to make way for a huge IKEA.

I really enjoyed my stay in Germany, even though I found that the local population had little in the way of a sense of humour, but I learned enough of the German language to get by. A big demob party was organised for me on the18[th] November 1961, the eve of my flight back from Wildenrath to Manston on the 19th. A journey undertaken with a thick head and nauseous stomach from another hangover and after travelling by train from Manston to Gloucester, and returning all of my now well-used kit, I was demobilised from RAF Gloucester on 20th November 1961.

In retrospect my two years National Service was immensely character building, which stood me in good stead for many of the challenges that would emerge in later life, I had enjoyed the travel and I never had any regrets about this period of my life.

CHAPTER SIX

The Swinging Sixties

I vividly remember my return to an un-regimented way of life on a sunny morning in civilian clothing with a travel warrant to New Street Station, where it had all started one year and 359 days earlier, a free man, returning to civilian way of life, my old mates and to start job hunting, at the start of the swinging sixties era, 6-5 special, Tommy Steel, Cliff Richards and Beatle Mania competing with the King in America, Elvis, who had preceded me serving part of his National Service in Germany.

I had been counting down the days to my demob and been looking forward to returning home to my old mates, football, cricket and a few pints with the lads, expecting things to be the same as when I left home two years earlier, only to find that everything had moved on, the guys had found girlfriends, some engaged. The football team was all new faces. Bill Drew was still completing his National Service in the Army at Catterick Camp in Yorkshire and there was nothing like the variety of life and buddies that I had enjoyed at Butz. It took several weeks to acclimatise to a very different way of life, but Mum and Dad were pleased to have their son and heir back home.

The great drain that I had been on the defence budget was at an end and I needed an income. The first advertisement that I saw for a heating engineer was at the Paragon Heating Company, based in Constitution Hill, Birmingham. I applied for the job and being the only applicant was appointed as a heating engineer, the wage was a princely sum of £12 per week. My first priority was transport and after receiving my first salary cheque, I had enough money for the 10% deposit required to purchase a red Austin Mini Van, the cheapest vehicle on the market; £254 (FOM 961) free of tax, because it was classed as a commercial vehicle. I should add that the heater and passenger seat were luxuries that were extra. This passion wagon may not have had the pulling power of a BMW but it was better than the bus. It is interesting to reflect that at that time, four weeks earning power, even at only £12 per week would provide sufficient income to put down the minimum 10% deposit on a car.

The Paragon Heating Company was progressive and expanding, it had a good client base; ABC Cinema Group used them exclusively in the Midland region, Cannings the Chemical Company had several factories in Birmingham that always required heating work and maintenance, and Mc. Kechnie Brothers, a big engineering group, were all companies that used Paragon exclusively. Additionally they would quote for schools, hospitals and any public buildings that were to be built.

The first enquiry that dropped on my drawing board was a tender for Nuneaton Police Headquarters and Magistrates Court. There was a debate by the directors whether to submit a quotation or not, as they thought it might be too big for them to handle, but it was from Warwickshire County Council and failure to quote may have resulted in other enquires being withheld from them.

I scrutinised the numerous drawings and specifications for over three weeks, taking off quantities sending out quotes for specialised equipment and finally arriving at a tender price over £26,000. In 1961, this was a very extensive project and the highest price ever quoted by the Paragon Heating Company. The company learned a month later that their quotation was the lowest and had been accepted, the worry was then, had something been missed out of the quotation, or had the labour been underestimated. After several days checking the estimate by Peter Dawson a director, it was deemed to be in order and correct.

For the next two years, I managed this project together with other smaller contracts to a profitable and successful conclusion, and a promotion to Technical Director followed, which sounds grand, but did not carry any real authority, though the salary was increasing rapidly with a £20 a week rise to £40 per week £2080 per annum.

The company was expanding rapidly, in fact too rapidly and moved into new premises in Henrietta Street near the central fire station. The premises were totally unsuitable and cracks began to appear in an unstable Board of Directors. A management consultant was appointed to sort out the declining balance sheet. This was despite a vast amount of very profitable work coming from ABC Cinema Group, which was going through great changes to stop the decline and closure of cinemas, caused by the greater availability of television.

All of their cinemas across the Midlands were to be converted from coal to oil fired boilers. Their Premier cinema in Birmingham 'The Bristol Cinema' Bristol Road was refurbished and converted to the new wide screen Cinemascope, reopening in record time with 'How the West was Won.'

It was later converted to a Ten Pin Bowling Centre. The Pavilion Wylde Green and the Pavilion in Stirchley were also totally refurbished and converted into Ten Pin Bowling Centres. These were all contracts that were very profitable, because the less time the cinemas were closed for conversion, was more important than the cost of refurbishment. A substantial amount of the work was carried out at very good day work and overtime rates. Incidentally, the Bristol Cinema was later demolished and is now a McDonald's

Reg Jervis, a tall, rotund, dominant captain of industry, was the man that had earlier been appointed to rescue an ailing company and I learned a great deal from this self appointed expert. He was reasonably astute, in that he recognised the problem was the company chairman, Bob Parsons, a perfect gentleman, immaculately turned out and breezed in every morning surrounded by a cloud of Old Spice aftershave, but his opulence in this aftershave was overshadowed by his lack of common sense. Bob had inherited the company from his father and he frequently underestimated projects and lost large sums of money completing them.

Mr. Jervis's solution to this problem was to expand the company further, so that it could keep the chairman in a style he had grown accustomed to, but at the same time keeping him away from day to day projects. His first objective was to generate increased turnover and profit, to the extent that the company could afford his own fees and Bob Parsons'. The addition of a full time salesman with car and expenses would also be required to generate more enquiries. The downside to this strategy, which Mr. Jervis may have failed to recognise, was the that the solid customer high profit margin projects previously mentioned were not easily expanded. Instead the expansion would come from local authority and hospital boards' highly competitive tenders being handled by new untried engineers.

In addition, the ratio of administration staff to engineering staff was growing out of all proportion. At that time there were six engineers preparing quotations and running contracts, which were generating the turnover and on the other hand had an accountancy and administration staff reporting to Reg Jervis, supposedly providing figures to check whether everything was going in the right direction, which was more than absorbing any additional profit by increased overheads.

The accountant Ian Craig, a nice guy but typical accountant, was building his own empire; purchase ledger clerk, sales ledger clerk, wages clerk, costing clerk, and an assistant accountant. His wife was also working as a comptometer operator checking quotations. Reg Jervis and the accountant were making the mistake many accountants make in not realising that the information being generated was all historical information and for a company in difficulty, this was much too late to rectify failings, particularly in contracting. It would also have meant that the management consultant would have to admit that his strategy was wrong. Control over overheads was vital and far more important than out of date reporting.

I could quickly see the fault lines in the company's direction and engineered a different niche for myself. Domestic warm air central heating was a cheap and easy to install method of heating and at the time Birmingham City Council were building 10,000 dwellings a year, all centrally heated by a basic warm air system. Everyone else in the company pooh poohed this route, as to them this wasn't engineering, it was small fry domestic heating. But I was always more commercially minded than intellectually principled, I had kept in close contact with Bill Drew, who was now working for West Midlands Gas Board (WMGB).WMGB were handling quotations for several local authorities with large building programmes for social housing within their regions.

My relationship with Bill was very rewarding for my career as, with Bill's help, I was able to secure several substantial contracts, 70 Flats for Halesowen Borough Council, 120 houses at Trent Valley Lichfield, 160 Houses at Woodgate Valley and 200 Houses at Stallings Lane, Kingswinford.

I had formed separate teams of fitters for this work, all working on piecework rates, so that labour costs could easily be controlled, plus better buying of materials due to the volume of units being handled. In fact this was the only profitable part of the company. I also recruited Ron Foster, a gas fitter from West Midlands Gas and Ron was my best fitter and the start of a very long relationship was emerging. Both Bill and I were playing cricket for West Midlands Gas, who had their own cricket ground in Holly Lane Erdington, and it was through Bill that I met my future wife.

CHAPTER SEVEN

Blind Date

Fate was soon to play a big part in my life shortly after Bill's demob from the Army, when Bill had met a nurse named Eileen. She was an Irish girl from Roscrea in Tipperary and was training to be a midwife at Selly Oak Hospital. On one particular occasion, which eventually turned out to be quite life changing for me, Bill and Eileen had been invited to a doctors leaving party at Willow Road, Edgbaston and they had a problem of too many nurses and not enough fellers. They asked me if I would risk a blind date with an Irish nurse Rita Nolan. In retrospect, the rather large space reserved on the shelf for me was getting bigger, as I was getting older with modest desperation I readily agreed.

I had sold the Mini Van and bought a brand new light grey Vauxhall Victor Saloon Car (JOC 918), which would surely have added to my pulling power. Not so. Rita stood me up and I never did meet Rita Nolan, but I did go to the party in Edgbaston and met another student midwife, a certain Joan Healy, also Irish, but from County Cork. We talked and danced and I offered her a lift back to the nurses home at Selly Oak and being the romantic that I was, I asked Joan if she would like to come out for the day on Sunday with Bill and me fishing. She explained that she was on night duty on Saturday night, but agreed to come as long as I didn't mind if she fell asleep.

Sunday arrived and we collected Joan from her home around 10 o'clock and being the perfect gentleman, I had packed a deckchair for Joan and a picnic lunch was all prepared. The river Severn at Bewdley was to be our destination, a picnic, on a beautiful hot sunny day, in a rural river location, what could be more romantic. The reality was that Joan fell asleep in the deck chair, was eaten by insects and was badly sun burned.

Joan must have been keen, because in spite of all her discomfort and my unique romantic style, she agreed to meet me the following weekend to go with Eileen to watch us play cricket at the British Gas Ground in Holly Lane, Erdington. It must have been a good summer, because again it was a pleasantly hot, sunny, cloudless day. Our team won and after a few celebratory drinks in the bar afterwards the girls were taken for chow mein and chopsticks to a Chinese restaurant in Hurst Street for dinner. The Wong Wing was about as far from Claridge's as you could get and probably not everyone's idea of a second date.

Over the next few weeks, my thirst for knowledge about this special young lady gathered momentum as I learned that she had been born on the 6th February 1938, the same year as me. Joan had grown up on a 38 acre farm on Cloughoula – More, Millstreet County Cork. She was the eldest of six, three brothers and two sisters and in addition to helping with milking cows as soon as she was old enough, she also had to look after the smaller siblings. Her first school was through the fields, to Cloughoula School and later to the Presentation Convent in Millstreet Town. In addition to her farming and child minding her mother was diabetic and needed help. Joan had been called from school once when her mother had passed out into a diabetic coma.

She had been awarded her leaving certificate after much studying and she had to find work. Although her family were considered relatively wealthy land owners in Ireland, in reality milking eleven cows and rearing a few pigs only just supported the family and there was little in the way of luxuries for this family with six growing children. The farm did not have a tractor so the work was carried out manually, with the help of three horses, Dandy, Foxy and Molly.

Joan's leaving certificate had not given her enough points for a teaching career and she had elected for nursing as her second choice, which meant that she would have to go to the North of Ireland, Belfast or England. Her mother Mamie would not hear of her going to Belfast.

Mamie spoke to a retired nurse, Sheila Manley, James the taxi driver's wife, and she recommended that she speak to a Mr. Vincent O'Sullivan, an eminent surgeon in London, who had originated from, and still returned regularly to the family home in Dernagree. Incidentally now the home of Jerry Pat the butcher. Doctor Vincent told Mamie that she would get very good training and care at his hospital, St. Anthony's, Cheam in Surrey and with his help and recommendation Joan was awarded a place as a student nurse.

She was seventeen and the furthest that she had travelled from home was to see her Uncle Bill Tarrant in Tipperary. The day of departure came and with tearful goodbyes to Mum, Dad, brothers and sisters, Joan left home, excited about the adventure that lay ahead, but with nervous anxiety, as she was rocked by the rhythm of the train from Millstreet via Limerick Junction and on to Dublin. She had arranged to meet up with another girl, who had also been accepted as a student nurse at the same hospital. After an overnight stay at her house, early next morning, she faced the unfriendly rolling Irish Sea and the ferry journey from Dublin to Holyhead, feeling very anxious and a little nauseous. Then on by train again, changing at Crewe and steaming on in to the metropolis. On leaving the train they were confronted by a web of coloured lines illustrating the underground system and with a little help from some friendly cockney's, they found their way to London Road, Cheam and their destination, St. Anthony's Hospital, which was to be her home for the foreseeable future.

After a few nervous days, she fitted into the disciplined routine of daily Mass before breakfast at 7am followed for the first three months in school, learning rules and procedures, before being allowed on to a ward. She was very homesick at first and missed her family, but with so many student nurses, mostly Irish, all being in the same predicament, they all quickly made friends and made the best of it, relying on weekly letters from home to keep her in touch with the family and news from Ireland.

St. Anthony's was and still is, a large private hospital, which cared for NHS patients, but had a large private wing, which cared for the very rich with Sheiks and VIPs travelling from all over the world for treatment there. At the time of Joan's arrival, all senior staff on the nursing side were nuns. It was to its very foundation a Catholic Hospital and met Mamie's requirements to the full. All nurses were strictly supervised and curfews were in force, for being allowed outside the hospital grounds at night was forbidden.

After passing her first year exam she travelled back home to Cloughoula, on holiday, flying for the first time, to the warmth and love of her family. Her younger brothers and sisters all wanted to know all about London and what the English people were like. It was such a wrench when the time came to leave home and take the flight back to St. Anthony's, she vowed not to return to Millstreet until her training was complete and then she would never leave home again. Her training and studying continued, with some relief at the Garry Owen and other Irish clubs in London at weekends. After passing the second year exams she was seconded to a sister hospital, St. Michael's Hospital at Hale in Cornwall, where she spent many happy months with sunshine, sea and A & E.

She returned to Cheam to do her final exams and become a state registered nurse. Joan hurried home after qualifying, but despite her earlier promise not to return to England, within a few weeks of country life she missed the lights of London and returned to St. Anthony's to become a theatre nurse and later theatre sister.

As time progressed, Joan together with a friend wanted more freedom from the strict regime at St' Anthony's and went flat hunting at a time when many Irish people seeking accommodation in London, were met with the sign 'No Dogs, No Irish'. This was before the influx of West Indian immigrants and at a time when the Black Maria, a police van, was referred to as the 'Paddy Wagon'.

But in spite of this blatant racism, they secured an affordable flat in Seven Sisters Road, Tottenham and she became a Tottenham Hotspur fan and spent many a Saturday afternoon shouting support for Danny Blanchflower, an Irish international football star at that time. His brother Jackie had been one of the Busby Babes that survived the Munich air crash.

Joan's next career move was to entail more studying, to acquire additional qualifications and she opted for midwifery training. Joan and her friend applied to Selly Oak Hospital in Birmingham and both were accepted. Their first impressions of Birmingham were not favourable but Selly Oak at that time was known as a good Midwifery Teaching Hospital. She then intended to return to London after qualifying as a midwife. Joan's friend was equally under whelmed with the Brummie accent and industrial atmosphere,

The Country Girl Pub in Raddlebarn Road did not have the same buzz that the Gary Owen Club had in London and at that time the clubs and pubs that now adorn Broad Street were few and far between.

Our meeting had given her some encouragement, as I was her only other friend outside the nurse's accommodation and we were growing very fond of each other. My new car provided essential transport in a town, which supported no underground tube service. In addition, it had very little nightlife compared with London. The relationship grew and when her friend returned to London after completing the first module of the midwifery course, Joan made a big break with her longstanding friend and stayed on to do her second part of midwifery at Lordswood Maternity Hospital, in Harborne, much to my delight and her friend's scorn saying, 'he will leave you before the course is finished.'

After Lordswood Hospital, Joan moved into nurses' accommodation in Moseley Hall and continued her training as a Pupil District Midwife in the deprived Balsall Heath Area of Birmingham. We would meet whenever Joan was off duty, often just driving out along the Hagley Road to the Gypsy's Tent pub, now the Badgers Set, where, in the long winter nights, there would be a welcoming open log fire blazing up the chimney.

Bill and Eileen's relationship was also blossoming and after a short romance and the ensuing engagement that followed, Bill asked me to be his best man for their wedding. They were to be married in Roscrea, Eileen's hometown in County Tipperary. My acceptance would lead me to Ireland for the first time. Flying from Elmdon airport, Birmingham to Dublin and then I travelled by bus from Dublin to Roscrea, a distance of 80 miles and seemed to take as long as a poor sermon, stopping at every lamp post if anyone wanted to get off, it stopped. If anyone wanted to get on it stopped, once for a woman carrying a small pig to the vet. It stopped for half an hour at a level crossing when passengers got off and chatted about Mrs. Murphy's new baby and she'd been only married for eight months. This first visit gave me an introduction to the Celtic pace of life and the magic of the rolling green fields, lakes and hills and a friendly relaxed lifestyle.

Joan missed me the few days that I was away, especially as I was enjoying Bill and Eileen's Irish wedding in her home country, while she was languishing in England trying to catch up on studies, in preparation for her final midwifery exam, which she went on to pass with flying colours and was now a state certified midwife. Joan Healy SRN SCM had a pleasant ring to it.

I told her about the amazing bus ride and how time seemed to standstill, she didn't think it was at all unusual and commented, 'Everyone knows it's a long way to Tipperary.' I thought there's no answer to that.

She then applied for a position as district midwife, and secured a post attached to Dudley Road hospital, covering the Winson Green Area of Birmingham, not one of the most affluent parts of the city and better known for its high security prison. The job came with a flat in Twining Road, off City Road; the accommodation was part of a large Victorian house, with two single flats on the first floor, one occupied by Joan the other occupied by another newly qualified midwife, Jean. The ground floor flat housed a married midwife and her husband.

I helped Joan with the move to her new home, a one bedroom flat, with a small kitchen and dining room. We also scoured local adverts in search of a second hand bicycle, vital transport to cover an area populated with many expectant mothers.

Joan, together with Jean and the married midwife were responsible for all of the prenatal, delivery and postnatal care for all home deliveries, day or night, for an area of about a two mile radius of Twining Road. Winson Green was a very densely populated area and most women opted for home delivery at that time, which kept Joan and her colleagues very busy, allowing little time for courting, or sleep, because she was permanently on call day and night, the only relief being annual leave or a rest day.

While Joan was climbing the nursing ladder of success my own career was also progressing I recognised that my position in the company was now very strong, I was generating and managing a substantial profitable turnover, which could have been lost if the Paragon Heating Company failed. In order to protect my position, I encouraged the accountant, Ian Craig, to put a joint proposal to Bob Parsons, the company chairman, that we should form a new company, Paragon Warm Air Systems Ltd.

Bob Parsons, Ian Craig and I were to be the owners of the new company, with equal shareholdings. The advantages were highlighted by Ian, by emphasising the scenario of, 'what if Tom left and did his own thing?' Bob Parsons reluctantly agreed to the formation of the new company.

I was now a full director of a company and despite only being a minority shareholder (33%) in fact I had all of the power as I had the contacts, technical expertise, and the business acumen to manage the contracts successfully, while using Paragon's administration services to get the new company off the ground. My salary increased and a company car was an additional prize.

I continued to secure large contracts, but now for the new company, two seventeen storey blocks of flats in Coventry, with 128 flats in each block, all fitted with warm air heating. The main contractor was British Lift Slab, a subsidiary of R. M. Douglas Construction. The buildings are now a monument to poor planning, but our performance on these projects was so successful, that two further identical blocks were negotiated on price rather than tender. Further contracts that were won were a 180 house project at Cheylesmore also in Coventry and 190 houses at Bedworth, Spooner's of Hull being the main contractor.

I would leave work each day, in my new company car, a dark green Ford Cortina Estate, to meet Joan at her Twyning Road flat. Our desire for each other was increasing, in fact, we were mad about each other.

Frequently I would ask Joan, 'What you would say if I asked you to marry me?'

'You will have to ask me to find out.' was always the same reply.

She was writing home weekly, telling her family all about this young man who was calling every day, her mothers probing replies were, 'what part of Ireland is he from, he is Catholic isn't he?' Unfortunately he was English, with a nomadic church history. This could have become a major problem, as Joan's Catholic faith and religion in her home was a very serious and important part of their lives. She avoided the issue for a while, writing to say that I had been to the Latin Mass with her at St. Patrick's Church, Dudley Road.

Joan never put me under any pressure to become a Catholic, but I could sense that it was important to her, I was quite relaxed after all, what did one more religion matter, they are all Christians. I started going to instruction to a Father Tom Murphy (related to the Murphy 'Tom the Dandy' who had a bar in Joan's home town). Father Murphy, a tall rather stout man, was Parish Priest at Our Lady of Lourdes Church in Yardley Wood and many months of discussion and debate followed. At least Joan could tell her parents that I was receiving instruction in the Catholic Faith.

Fr. Murphy at our Lady of Lourdes with choir and pupils from Yardley Wood Junior School

After several delayed attempts the day was approaching for Joan to meet my parents. It's difficult to say who was the most anxious, my mother, who had had some teeth removed and was left with a badly bruised face and was about to meet a foreign Catholic nurse who was creating distance between her and her only precious son, of whom she was very proud.

Joan on the other hand, who although very proud of her nationality, was aware that the trouble in Northern Ireland had given many English people a jaundiced view of Irish people at that time, as well as being rather shy quiet person, who desperately wanted to make a good impression on my family. So, dressed to the nines and after a few Hail Mary's at the morning Mass, she was well prepared for the ordeal ahead.

The occasion was a nervous Sunday afternoon tea. My mother had gone to a lot of trouble to impress, with delicate sandwiches and home made cakes. After a stuttering start with a few pregnant pauses, it generally went well and they and my sister Connie quickly came to care for and respect Joan. It was generally agreed that she was a good influence on me. However, Joan did not really feel at home, which was not completely overcome until she had the security of marriage.

The pressure was now on me to meet Joan's parents, Dan and Mamie, also her devoutly Catholic family. Holidays were arranged and a flight booked. I had no idea what to expect, with thoughts of my earlier trip to Tipperary. I had always lived in a town and had grown up with an only sister and I was on my way to a small farm, in a rural community, in a different country, not only to meet Joan's parents, but five younger brothers and sisters. Keen to make a good impression I was dressed in a smart suit, white shirt, red tie and highly polished shoes.

Dan had hired James Manley's taxi to meet and collect us at the airport, a round trip of eighty miles and on first sight they thought I had the appearance of a solicitor or bank manager.

The journey from Cork, travelling along the Lea Valley, through a patchwork of ploughed fields all various shades of green fields with cows grazing lazily, the journey was interrupted with a stop at the Castle Hotel in Macroom, where Dan invited me to join him for a pint of beer. Joan and her mother stayed in the car, as it was not the done thing in those days for women to be seen in a bar. I returned the compliment to Dan and two pints later we left, after a conversation fragmented with misunderstandings caused by the differences in the Birmingham and Cork accents, to rejoin the ladies who had been left waiting patiently in the car with the driver. This had appeared very strange to me, but I was learning the Irish customs by the minute.

Over the remaining twelve miles to Clougoula-More, the terrain changed and became more rocky and hilly, as we approached Joan's home with Clara Mountain coming into view, all in quiet contemplation. The car turned into a narrow boreen and rolled on into the farmyard, to be welcomed by Rose, an Irish sheep dog, barking and to shouts of 'he's here' almost as if it was the Pope himself that had been expected. I felt like a species from another planet, as I was introduced to Paddy, Dennis, Nora, Kathleen and youngest brother Donie.

On entering the house via a small back kitchen, which housed a cooking range and sink units, I was standing on a flagged stone floor and looking I up saw a wooden, boarded ceiling bearing many coats of paint and hanging from the ceiling hooks were parcels wrapped in newspaper and tied with string. To my amusement I thought, could these be the remains of previous unsuccessful suitors?

A peat fire kindling in the large open grate, with steam rising from a kettle hanging from a hook over the fire, had a welcome homely feel about it. I later discovered that the parcels hanging from the ceiling were home cured fitches of bacon.

However, my embarrassment was only in its infancy, the two pints of beer were now weighing heavily on my bladder and on asking, 'Where's the toilet?' I was met with a stony silence and after a pause and some giggling, I pointed out to Joan that my predicament

TOM GRAINGER

was getting more acute by the minute I was then,
with much relief, directed to the forty acre field. In
fact there was a hut above the haggard, with a seat and
a bucket and paper on a hook, for ones more solid
needs.

The Irish hospitality was only just beginning as Dan
poured me a tot of Potcheen, a locally brewed spirit,
made in the mountains and because of its illegality,
reputedly made by the fairies. Not wishing to be a wimp,
I accepted gratefully, but with some regret when it hit the
back of my throat; I became speechless and tears were
running down my cheeks, much to the humour of Joan,
who had some idea of the strength of this spirit, and her
brothers and sisters.

When the burning in my throat had subsided and my
glazed eyes cleared, I thought I was seeing an apparition
as I gazed at the Sacred Heart picture above a small red
lamp with a flickering flame. This had been hung in a
place of prominence on the wall backing onto the
staircase.

On the opposite side of the staircase via a small
hallway was the parlour; a spacious room with a large
table, which could seat ten or twelve people, on the right
was an equally imposing, ornately carved dresser with
a large mirror housing china ware. To the left was a
wrought iron fireplace with an old picture of some
distant relative above and in the corner an antique
windup gramophone.

The table had been set for four places, with the best
china, cold meat platters, ham and chicken, tomatoes,
homemade bread, butter, jam and fruit cake. I found
later that this room was normally reserved for the Priest,
when the Healy's were hosting the Stations in their

home. Dan, Mamie, Joan and I sat down to a somewhat formal tea and were waited on by Joan's sisters Nora and Kathleen, who couldn't help themselves from sniggering nervously.

I desperately needed some space, to relax from the nervous pressures of the day and arranged with Joan to go out for the evening, there was a dance that night at the Star Ballroom and this was an ideal escape. I was directed to my room, to unpack and wash and freshen up and only shortly later, I could hear mumbling chanting sounds from below, Ha..l, Ma.y, Mo t r of God, Ho.y Mar. Mo.. God, which seemed to go on forever, I was totally mystified by this rhythmic poetic ritual, but I was reluctant to go back down stairs to disrupt what might have been a witches spell being cast on me. Joan later explained that they were saying the Rosary and it was nothing to do with my presence, she explained that it happened every night and no one could go out until after five decats of the Rosary had been recited by the whole family that were present.

The Star Ballroom, which was on our nearside of Millstreet Town, was a two mile walk downhill, needless to say the same distance back up, it just seemed further. The ballroom was best featured in the film, 'The Ballroom of Romance'. It was an amazing spectacle, all the single girls on the left of the room and all the single fellers on the right, when the music started there was a stampede and the lucky ones finished up with partners of some description or other. The ones already partnered could view this maelstrom with a certain amount of relief and satisfaction. The band, an Irish Show Band, was very popular and the floor was soon bouncing to the beat of Hucklebuck and other pop tunes of the day. I was not much of a dancer and never destined to audition for Riverdance, we spent little time dancing and I welcomed the time with Joan, just comparing the experiences of the day, in good humour.

The following morning I was as usual awake early and arose to see the cows coming down from the upper fields to be milked, with Rose barking at their hooves. I waited awhile before getting up, hoping that Joan would also rise early to give me some support, as I was still mystified by some of the protocol; after having been shushed from speaking while the Angelis was being strictly observed by her mother.

Joan was determined to enjoy a well-earned sleep in, so safely chaperoned by two sisters, I finally ventured downstairs and went in to the yard visually exploring from the doorway. To the left I could see the hut, which housed the loo and beyond was a chicken coop with hens out free range, pecking about the grass and further down still was the haggart, in which carrots, onions, parsnips and cabbages were being grown, encompassed with wire netting protecting the crops from the hens and rabbits, potatoes and turnips were grown on a much bigger scale in a field above the boreen. Also in the yard were guinea fowl, turkeys and geese and higher up to the right were the pig sties.

I was now more casually dressed, and waiting for Joan's arrival for breakfast when Dan and all the boys came in from milking and hunger was much more important than the English newcomer, the atmosphere was much more relaxed, with many questions about the differences between England and Ireland being exchanged. The boys wanted to know what time I milked in England and I had to admit that I thought that the milk came from the supermarket, it was an exaggeration, but it made the boys laugh.

The few days that were left were spent meeting other relatives, some American cousins from San Fransisco were over visiting and they gave us the loan of their hired car to tour Killarney. The love for Ireland that I had absorbed from my earlier trip to Tipperary was enhanced and multiplied after seeing Killarney, a fondness, which is still engraved on the whole of my personality today.

The time came to return to the airport and to reflect on the warmth and affection that I had received from the Healy family, the fun with Joan's brothers and sisters, and the hospitality that Ireland had offered in its own unique way.

I returned to work to find that as quickly as Paragon Warm Air Systems success was growing, Paragon Heating's fortunes were declining under the weight of high overheads and poor management. In an effort to reduce the overheads they moved to new, more suitable and less costly premises in Adderley Road, Saltley. Paragon Warm Air Systems completed the move with them and shared the rent and rates also making a contribution to administration costs, but I was under no illusion that the road ahead could well bring a bumpy ride.

It was while contemplating the future responsibilities of both work and what married life would bring, and sitting in an armchair in front of the fire with the television sounds in the background, that my thoughts were interrupted by a newsflash. An assassination attempt had been made on President Kennedy's life and within an hour it was confirmed that the shooting had claimed his life. I wondered selfishly what effect this would have on the stability of the world peace.

CHAPTER EIGHT

Engaged to Wed

Soon after our return to Birmingham, I knew that I wanted to marry Joan. I went shopping for an engagement ring and I had intended to wait for a romantic dinner at the weekend to chance a proposal, but the ring was burning a hole in my pocket and when I arrived at the flat in Twining Road that evening, I, in a very excited and anxious state, almost blurted out my proposal and asked, 'Will you marry me?' She was so surprised that this was an actual proposal that she hesitated, until she saw the ring and then hugged me with delight and said, 'Yes'.

Over the next few weeks and following Christmas 1964, budgets were calculated, and plans made and it was decided that if our spending was cut to a minimum, we could save enough for a deposit on a house 10% (£350) plus the cost of a seven day honeymoon in Ireland and the minimum of furniture. We calculated that one thousand pounds was required, which could be saved in ten months and the wedding date was set for the 14th October 1965 and St. Patrick's Church in Millstreet was booked. Joan's parents had insisted on paying for an Irish wedding, much to our relief, as the budget was petty tight although my parents did want to contribute to the cost.

The wedding planning was only just underway when a special news bulletin announced the death of Sir Winston Churchill, this great man, possibly the greatest Englishman of the twentieth century, was to receive a State Funeral. He had been the First Sea Lord during World War I and had led England to victory in World War II, while standing alone for two years against the might of Hitler's Nazi Regime. In addition he had been awarded a Nobel Prize for Literature. The television pictures showing him lying in state in Westminster Hall and the procession surrounding the gun carriage carrying the coffin to St Paul's Cathedral was a moving sight and a well-earned tribute to a great man.

My instruction in Catholicism was completed and I was baptised and had taken my first confession and Holy Communion, which was celebrated with great joy with Bill and Eileen. But it was not received with the same joy and excitement in my parent's home, which surprised me, because my parent's failure to attend church had not dulled their concerns about the Catholic Church, which they saw as a money grabbing institution. In all honesty, 50 years on, they were fairly accurate in their assessment and although I am still a devout Catholic I often refer to the Catholic Church as the church of the second collection.

Because the wedding was to take place in Ireland, documentation had to be sorted out between my Parish, now St. Margaret Mary, Perry Common Road, The Bishop of Birmingham and Joan's Parish in Ireland, the Millstreet Parish and the Bishop of Kerry. In addition, the banns had to be read in both parishes. All of my relatives were visited and invitations given out and much to my surprise, most of my aunts, uncles and cousins from my mother's side accepted. Most of the aunts and uncles on my father's side hardly kept in touch with each other since my grandfather's death, three years earlier in December 1961, and were reluctant to travel so far to their nephew's wedding.

At the end of September, Joan delivered her last baby in Winson Green, by this time she weighed just over six and a half stone from working long hours without sleep and cycling everywhere, complete with delivery bag and gas and air machine strapped on the back of her bicycle. She had enjoyed the work very much, but the responsibility of two lives, mother and baby, at a time when few homes had telephones and any emergencies were much more stressful with blue lights flashing to Dudley Road Hospital, often on a life saving journey. She handed in her notice and left district midwifery for married life.

She returned to Ireland by air for the last time as a spinster, ten days before me, to help with the wedding arrangements. I followed with my parents and sister by car and ferry arriving the day before the wedding. My parents had not met Dan and Mamie until the day before the wedding. I had played virtually no part in the wedding planning and preparations and was not at all sure what to expect. My parents, sister and aunts, uncles and cousins were staying at B&B's in Millstreet Town, the Wallis Arms was not a residential hotel at that time.

They were just as confused by the Cork accent as I had been earlier. The novelty of country life and a different culture was experienced with mixed feelings of pride and consternation, about their only son's marriage.

Dan and Mamie were probably equally concerned that their eldest daughter was about to commit the rest of her life to what might have been a descendent from Black and Tans.

The night before the wedding I was despatched to Aunt Madge's in Cullen to sleep to ensure that Joan was not seen until we met at the alter the next day. As I walked up the long aisle to be greeted by the Priest, I wondered in amusement how the church did not topple over, as I saw Mum, Dad, and my sister, one aunt, one uncle and three cousins on my side of the church and the rest of Millstreet on the other, with all of my side standing up, kneeling down and sitting down a few seconds after everyone else and sometimes not at all. Joan's passage up the aisle on her father's arm to be given to away to me was also a journey into the unknown for her, but was the start of an unbelievably happy and loving relationship.

We were eventually pronounced man and wife, the nuns who had taught Joan at the Presentation Convent had played the organ and sang angelically in this magnificent church, beautifully decorated with floral decorations, which was later described by an English Priest as having Cathedral qualities. All of which had provided the foundation for our married life together and was the bedrock for an unbelievable relationship, which lasted, till death do us part, over forty years and four children later.

The morning of the wedding was a wet and rather miserable day and no photographs were taken outside the church. My cousin Terry was the official photographer and was reluctant to get his expensive equipment wet. Neily (Cornelius) Healy, Joan's uncle, drove us at almost a walking pace to the Lake Hotel in

Killarney for a reception of about sixty guests. He drove so slowly I thought the soup would be cold. Paddy, Joan's brother, was my best man assisted by Dennis, my groomsman. After the Wedding Breakfast and speeches of welcome, and thanking everyone for coming and their gifts, the day brightened up, the sun came out and beautiful photographs were taken with the Lakes of Killarney in the background.

The reception would have been very modest by today's standards, the emphasis being on the sacrament of marriage celebrated by a meal with friends and relatives and finished at six o'clock in the evening without music or dancing, much to our delight. The very happy couple heaved a big sigh of relief and drove off, covered in confetti and tin cans tied to the rear of the Vauxhall Victor, heading for the Eccles Hotel in Glengarriff, which overlooked the Atlantic Ocean. The rest of the honeymoon passed in a glazed shroud of joy and happiness, travelling to Garnish Island and various beauty spots around Kerry. We allowed just enough time for one last trip home to Cloughoula, to say goodbye to Mum, Dad, brothers and sisters and then on to the ferry and back to a new life together in England.

We arrived home to number 64 Hazelwood Road, Streetly, having completed the house purchase just one week before Joan left for Ireland, the cost £3,250. We had to pay a fee to the solicitor up front, together with a deposit of £325, It was not easy to secure a mortgage of £3000 despite having an annual salary in excess of £2500. Building societies were only lending to existing savers and Aldridge and District Council came to the rescue, with a loan 1/8th % above the going rate of 7%. In addition I took out a with profits endowment policy, to give protection to Joan, should anything happen to me. I paid £35 per quarter for the 25 year term of the mortgage, giving additional life cover for the cost of the house. This proved to be a very sound investment 25 years later, maturing with a handsome pay out.

Our only possessions consisted of a Neworld radiation gas cooker, a wedding present from Mum and Dad, a new double bed, which we had purchased out of our £1000 wedding, honeymoon and house budget, a travelling trunk belonging to Joan, which used as a table and two casual chairs which, were a present from Connie, in addition to wedding presents that we had received from our wedding guests. All of the hall and the two reception rooms were polished parquet flooring and the kitchen had plastic floor tiles. The rear reception room had a patio door opening out onto a small lawned garden, with an imitation wishing well near the bottom boundary fence.

Our plan was that I would go to work and earn the money, Joan would stay at home and have babies, she had grown up with several brothers and sisters and my only sister had never seemed quite enough. I was old fashioned even then, but believed that it was my responsibility to support my wife and family something that is not remotely possible today. However, after eighteen months and no sign of babies, Joan believed that she was wasting all of the training that she had undertaken and it was mutually agreed that she would go back to work. A vacancy was advertised for a sister midwife at Portland House, Wednesbury, a GP maternity unit, which she applied for and was appointed.

I had retained the Vauxhall Victor (JOC 318), now referred to as Jock, although I was mainly driving the company car, it was decided that Joan should learn to drive, to enable her to take 'Jock' to work and not have to rely on an irregular bus service. Joan was not a natural driver and it is fair to say that husbands teaching their wives to drive would put a strain on even the most perfect of relationships. However, our love for each other and Joan's patience with me navigated us through some testing situations. Joan went on to pass the test first time, after a few additional professional lessons.

The Paragon Heating Company's fortunes were not improving and their move to new premises had not gone very far in reducing their overheads. Lending by the banks was very tight as I had found in seeking a mortgage, their cash flow was deteriorating, which was impinging on the Warm Air Company, as money was being borrowed to prop up the parent company and finally when they were having difficulty in drawing the wages from the bank, they called in a liquidator on the advice of their auditors.

This was quite a set back and brought about a period of uncertainty as my marriage was in its infancy and I had to support a new wife, an equally new mortgage and a cocktail of other bills. But I had seen it coming and was delighted that Paragon Warm Air Systems was a separate entity, with different shareholders and different directors. Bob Parsons was devastated at the loss of his fathers company and resigned his directorship in the Warm Air Company and transferred his shares to me, to help preserve his dented reputation within the heating industry and enable him to face the creditors with a clearer conscience. He was one of life's gentlemen, although sadly not equipped for the commercial world.

The liquidation was a traumatic experience and although I was only on the fringe of the auction of assets and creditors meeting, I was still concerned that some of the old Paragon misfortunes would adhere itself to my company, but it was all part of a learning curve, as my own company management expertise was still in its youth and it was all good experience, which had to be called on much later in life.

CHAPTER NINE

The Budding Entrepreneur

I was now standing on my own two feet. I started by negotiating with the landlord to stay in the same premises and arranged to rent the first floor only, at a reduced figure and with it reduced rates. Paragon Warm Air Systems could not support a salary for an accountant and Ian Craig had secured a good position at the Hanger Motor Company, a main Ford Dealership. Joan started to do the bookkeeping, an extra subject she had taken at school.

John Giles had joined me at Paragon earlier, after leaving the Gas Board at Lichfield where he had been working as a salesman, but had a technical background and experience of the warm air business. He had kept Warm Air Systems ticking over while I was up to my neck in nuptials, and he stayed on after the Paragon collapse. Ron Foster was still my leading fitter and could be relied on to jump to any emergency or crisis that occurred. The warm air business was very buoyant with a high demand for housing in a busy private sector and even bigger demand for social housing in the public sector. Bill Drew was still giving me as much help as possible and on arrival of Bill and Eileen's first child,

Joan had been asked to be Godmother, a task which she accepted with great delight.

As the company gradually emerged out of the shadow cast by the old Paragon's failure and the business gained strength with cash flow improving each month and as all the profits generated were available for the company and were not being diluted by its now defunct parent company. One of our biggest problems that we were encountering was procuring the sheet metal ductwork that was required for coupling the warm air heating boiler to the outlet grilles. Our main supplier was unreliable and often our fitters would be left standing and wasting valuable time, waiting for ductwork that had been promised by Mad Mick. He was so named because of his Irish origin and the company's name Modern Air Duct. MAD's products invariably arrived late or not at all, which was in contrast to his most imaginative excuses, which were in abundance.

I decided that the solution was to make our own sheet metal ductwork. I formed another company Midland Metal Fabrications Ltd, the idea being initially to manufacture ductwork for my own Warm Air Company, secondly to manufacture for any other company that was having difficulty sourcing sheet metal products and thirdly to expand the business, eventually into other metal fabrications. I also knew that this would give me two strings to my bow and if the demand for warm air systems declined, the long term protection and providing for my wife and family was always at the forefront of my mind and any form of insurance cover was better than none. This was to prove a particularly wise move as things turned out much later.

The existing premises were not at all satisfactory for manufacturing, being on the first floor, but as I was working on an almost non-existent budget, a move to other premises was out of the question. There was sufficient space at the Adderley Road location and I started by scouring the newspapers for machinery auctions, Stevens Champion and Slater were specialists in this field. I made successful bids at the auction, and bought a four-foot treadle guillotine, a four-foot hand folder, and a spot welding machine for very little outlay.

I made a trap door in the floor and then a hoist was secured to the stout ceiling joists and we hauled the newly acquired machinery into place, to the sound of creaking joists and well out of sight of Health and Safety officials, which were not as prominent then as they are now. I bought my first ton of six foot by three foot 24g galvanised sheet steel for £70 and hauled it up manually sheet-by-sheet, up through the trap door. By employing two youngsters on low wages and having worked out all of the cutting sizes for them, I worked along side them, thereby learning the trade, while teaching the trainees at the same time. It is interesting, as I reminisce about the past, how many start up companies today would do so, with such little resources and in such primitive conditions.

This was obviously a very testing time, starting a new manufacturing company and running a busy expanding contracting company simultaneously, with only the help of John Giles and Joan doing the books at home, and this prompted me to employ a junior to type invoices, statements and answer the telephone when either John or I were out of the office. I always believed that the key to success was low overheads. I had seen many failures of the companies with flashy office blocks and luxury cars and in the case of the old Paragon, too many chiefs and not enough Indians.

Working very hard and long hours to keep many balls in the air at the same time had caused me to become unhappy that I still had another shareholder, Ian Craig, who was making no effort or contribution to the growth of the company, but would gain from my labours more and more as the company grew.

Paragon Warm Air Systems had a net asset value at that time of £4,800. This may not seem to be a great deal in the way of assets, but bearing in mind my house had only cost £3,250, it puts it in perspective. I offered to buy Ian's 33% share for £1,600. Ian being an accountant would know that if he did not accept, the contracting profits could well find their way into the manufacturing business if he refused. Ian agreed to accept the offer. After all he had gained £1,600 without making any investment originally. The shares in both companies were then divided 51% for me and 49% Joan.

At home, in my near nonexistent spare time, I was decorating rooms in order of priority and furniture was being added with each pay cheque, a telephone had been installed and with the arrival of a television set to while away the winter nights, it was the right time to invite Dan and Mamie over to England to see where Joan lived. Their visit would only last for a week as cows still had to be milked and animals fed while they were away and it was to be the only time that Mamie ever came to England. She was very happy to see that Joan was being looked after like a lady and had a comfortable centrally heated home, no Wellington boots and milking cows every day, but disappointed that there was still no sign of her first grandchild. On a shopping trip into the Bull Ring, I was about to buy a mother in laws tongue plant for Joan, but her mother insisted on making the purchase. That plant prospered, survived being split several times and lasted much of our life together and became almost a monument to Mamie.

We always looked forward to our summer holidays in Ireland every year, I was working long hours and particularly Joan, as she was a little isolated in Streetly with few friends and missed her parents and family. I was mad about Ireland, a totally different way of life and during early visits I tried helping out with haymaking and the like, but the boys told me I was much too soft for farming and had many laughs at my expense. I remember one humorous episode when Joan, who had grown up with horses was riding Foxy, a chestnut Mare, bareback wearing a skirt, when Paddy, Joan's brother, gave the horse a whack across the flanks with a stick and Joan galloped off down two fields, before bringing the horse to a canter. I also received a shock that evening when it came to saying the Rosary, Mamie in her wisdom declared that I would say the fourth decat.

The following year we took my uncle with us. Jim, a very keen fisherman, had been dropping broad hints about wanting to fish in Ireland and as there was plenty of room in the car for the journey and for the ferry crossing, he came with us. The B&I ferries in those days were more like cargo ships, and most likely under British Rail control. Hygiene and cleanliness were not a high priority on the ferry and it would not be uncommon to fight off the flies to finish a meal before the flies had had their share and it reminded Joan of the first awful and anxious journey that she had made to England more than a decade before.

At this time at the Fishguard Port there was no roll on roll off ferries and the car had to be craned on and off with net slings under the front and rear wheels and then lowered into a hold with other cargo. We all enjoyed a smooth crossing and the traditional Irish rain avoided County Cork for most of the two weeks, affording us some fine weather fishing in the rivers Lea and Blackwater, while Joan visited her numerous relations and enjoyed time with her family.

Jim stayed at Mrs. Rogan's house, 'Morelands', a B&B in Church Street on the approach to Millstreet Town and would hitch a lift to the farm on the horse and cart with Paddy, when he returned from the Creamery to rejoin both Joan and me. Jim was delighted with the hospitality that he enjoyed with Mrs. Rogan and commented about having fresh cream on his cornflakes, before a full Irish breakfast, which usually included black and white pudding.

Late autumn, after returning from holiday in 1968, Joan excitedly told me that I was at last to become father, the happy news was relayed to Ireland by letter and Mamie was overjoyed at the news that her first, so eagerly awaited grandchild was on its way. Dan would become a Granddad and brothers and sisters would be aunts and uncles, a new first time experience for them all.

However, sadly on the 19th February 1969 Mamie died suddenly. Willie Leary, the grocer where Kathleen, Joan's sister worked, waited until I arrived home from work. Shrove Tuesday was very early that year and I had just finished consuming my pancakes soaked in lemon juice and sugar when the telephone rang. I took the telephone call at six thirty in the evening, advising me of the devastating news.

Joan was in the next room and I had no option but to break the shattering news without delay, she was by now six months pregnant and was inconsolable that her Mum would not see her longed for grandchild. I telephoned the doctor explaining the situation and asked for sedatives for the journey that lay ahead. The only early flight available the next day was from Birmingham to Dublin and after a broken night's sleep we awoke early to find that it had snowed quite heavily overnight.

Clearing enough snow to get off the steep drive, we hurried on to the airport. Our sombre arrival led to more consternation when we discovered that most flights were being cancelled to many destinations, but our Guardian Angel allowed us on the last flight out of Birmingham that morning. Our arrival at Dublin was greeted with sunshine and a clear runway, we hastily cleared customs and made a bee line for the Hertz car hire desk, renting an Austin Mini to make our way south with good road conditions.

The further south we travelled, the darker the clouds became and before we reached Mallow, we ran into a snowstorm and the further we progressed, so did the blizzard. By the time we arrived in Mallow the snow was six inches deep and in our haste to get to Millstreet we skidded off the road between Mallow and the Sandpit House, but the light weight of the mini and in blind desperation I lifted the rear of the car out of the ditch and we were able to continue our disconsolate and perilous journey.

We arrived at St. Joseph's Hospital Mortuary in Millstreet at roughly eight thirty that night, to see a large crowd muttering, 'They're here'. Dan and the family had delayed the closure of the coffin until Joan arrived to say her last goodbyes and to be left only with sadness and an abundance of childhood memories.

All too soon after our arrival Joan's mother was taken by hearse to be received into St. Patrick's Church to the familiar lyrical chanting devotion of the Rosary. This Rosary gathered a depth of meaning at this devastating time and quite suddenly gave time for reflection after our hectic and exhausting journey. We eventually arrived back at the farm after the Rosary to a bleak, cold, desolate building, feeling numb and no one quite knowing what to say, as everyone was in shock and inconsolable.

After a sleepless night, the family prepared for the Requiem Mass. No one ate breakfast. The snow was still falling. I tried to keep busy doing the practical things, like lighting the range and a fire in the parlour. The cold was intense, partly from the low temperatures and partly from the state of shock, cold drafts seemed to come from all directions, all compounded by a building with little or no insulation that had been built many years before by Dan's forefathers to a very basic standard. The Requiem Mass was a sombre interlude and a prelude to the internment, with all mourners holding umbrellas as a shield against the cutting wind and driving snow. This was to become more hysterical with Joan having to restrain her sister Kathleen, so demented with grief that she wanted to throw herself into the grave. The snow continued unceasingly for the next two days creating a Christmas card, bleak winter setting for Wuthering Heights, from which our only escape was with the assistance of the recently acquired farm tractor.

I decided that it was not in Joan's interest, or the unborn baby, to stay longer in these Arctic and isolated conditions and made the hazardous two mile journey into Millstreet to book a flight from Cork to Birmingham, departing the next day. Saying our farewells in an atmosphere shrouded in gloom and sadness and leaving, with our hire car being towed by the tractor, until we found better road conditions near Carriganimmy, then on to Cork returning the damaged Mini to the rental company at the airport. Even the return flight was a disaster, due to the plane being diverted from Birmingham to London and in the rush that followed to catch the next train, with tickets provided by Aer Lingus, Joan experienced acute abdominal pain, as she collapsed on to a rail carriage seat, with the train pulling out of Euston Station. However, the pain subsided as she gradually relaxed in exhaustion, to the drumming rhythm of train on rail.

In addition to the worry of leaving her family in such a forlorn state, she was also worrying about the health of our baby, which from one view point had the advantage in that she had something else on which to focus. The post journey visit to the doctor confirmed that all was well. Communication and consolation with her family was only by letter as there was still no telephone at the farm.

On the 8th July 1969, Joan went into a long and extended labour, which, after hours and hours of labour pains, worry and anguish, we were told that the baby was becoming distressed and they would perform a caesarean section, 'Don't worry,' said the surgeon 'I'll have the baby out in ten minutes.' Joan warned me that if anything happened I was to baptise the baby myself. Joanne Mary entered the world as promised ten minutes later, on 9th July, in fine voice. I said that she was roaring for me, but I may have been biased.

The new addition to our family at Hazelwood Road brought the usual sleepless nights, but Joan's experienced midwifery hands helped with the practical side while I was barely able to cuddle nervously my new pride and joy. The baptism was arranged and Joan was delighted when she knew that Nora and Dan had agreed to fly over and would be Godparents to our first born, an event that helped with the grieving process, which still hung very heavily in all of our hearts.

I returned to work with an extra mouth to feed and less income coming in as Joan had again given up nursing to concentrate on her own little paediatric baby Joanne a labour of love which was to be very demanding, but we worked hard at sharing our love three ways, which later became six ways and to a uniquely close and loving family.

Work on a new town outside Northampton at Wellingborough was well underway and J.S. Wright Ltd. a well established heating engineering company in Birmingham, had secured the contract from the main contractor Marriot and Co., for the heating and plumbing for 500 houses I canvassed them to supply the ductwork for their project and after they had been let down by Mad Mick, they gave the order to Midland Metal Fabrications Ltd., which enabled me to feed manufactured supplies to the site weekly.

Both of my small companies were now growing rapidly, both in turnover and profit. Paragon Warm Air Systems, the contracting company, had narrowly missed out on a tender for John Mowlem Construction for another phase of 500 Houses at Wellingborough, but a few weeks into the contract the sub contractor went into liquidation. They contacted Paragon. Did we have the capacity to take over the contract and would our original tender price still hold? The answer to both questions was yes. I travelled to the site to meet the Mowlem surveyor and we agreed the costs for finishing off the work in progress on the first 20 houses that had been started by the previous sub contractor and contracts for the whole project were signed.

Midland Metal Fabrications Ltd. the manufacturing company was now supplying ductwork on a weekly basis to two extensive sites in Wellingborough together with our other customers and it was now imperative that larger manufacturing premises would have to be found. We quickly located low cost premises and the move to the more spacious factory in Sheepcote Street ensued.

The premises were not ideal, but they were affordable and on the ground floor, access was down a long passageway, wide enough for our own truck and cars, but difficult for big lorries delivering steel. We purchased additional machinery and updated some existing equipment, a six foot power guillotine was purchased at auction and a hand guillotine and hand presses were again all added to our assets by bidding at auction.

The expression feast or famine came into our minds, because after waiting nearly four years for Joanne to arrive, it was no time before another baby was on the way. The news coincided with the arrival of an invitation by Nora, Joan's sister to her and Mick Twomey's wedding. The combination of the new pregnancy and the necessity to travel again rekindled memories of the last time this partnership came together. However, holiday cover was organised and ferries booked for another joyous family event.

The journey was hardly underway, before some of the earlier trepidation was soon well founded, as a series of mishaps gathered momentum at an unbelievable pace. Our wedding quest, taking us firstly to the Fishguard ferry, started to run into trouble before we had reached Ross on Wye, when the temperature gauge in the Ford Cortina started to reach the danger zone, warning us of an engine cooling problem. I said, 'Well that's a great start,' the fan belt had snapped and we changed our route to take the shortest, Head of the Valleys road and limping from garage to garage, frequently stopping to top up the overheating radiator with water.

At each stop we begged for a mechanic to fit a new fan belt, eventually arriving at a garage deep in the Welsh countryside, where we found a sympathetic mechanic who agreed to do the repair while I urged him to do it as quickly as possible, because we had to catch the ferry.

The mechanic in a broad Welsh accent, uttered the shattering news 'Sorry Boyoh there's no rush you know, the stevedores are on strike, so no ferries will be sailing tonight!'

'This must be a cunning Welsh hoax' I thought, as I accelerated to the ferry with all haste, trying to make up for lost time, only to find that the mechanic's news had been accurate, the unions had given up talks with the employers and would not resume until 8am the next day.

Now, while the ferry port was busy with daily crossings to Rosslare the town of Fishguard at this time was like a cemetery with lights. The impression that the Welsh watched Coronation Street in bed was enhanced by the lack of human existence. We even had difficulty in finding a fish and chip shop to provide sustenance, let alone a restaurant. In fairness my view may have been jaundiced by the experiences of the day, which had exaggerated my long-term problem with the Welsh people, who would switch to speaking Welsh on hearing an English voice and it was not being enhanced in Fishguard.

Eventually we found a B&B that would house the two of us plus baby for the night and after a fitful sleep with baby in the middle, we ate a substantial breakfast while Joanne was devouring her bottle. We returned to the ferry port, to find that the unions were consulting their members and talks would resume again at 11.00 am. 'Up you the customers, we want our rights,' was getting little sympathy from me. An announcement was made at 2pm that the ferry would sail at 6pm, but only passengers would be transported, no cars would be loaded. The Welsh were sinking lower and lower on my Christmas card list. It is not surprising that most of the mines were closed followed by a very modern steelworks with this Trade Union dogma.

If it had not been for the dangling carrot of Nora's wedding, we would have given up at that stage, but we were both blessed with a dogged determination to be there for Nora's big day. We checked to see if flights from Cardiff or Bristol would ease our plight, but without success, and we returned into Fishguard Town, consumed a late lunch, bought another suitcase, and repacked the luggage. Most of the baby necessities had been thrown in the back of the car, which was now to remain at the port.

I sought out the most important official I could find and explained my predicament, a wife who was quite obviously six months pregnant, a nine-month-old baby and with more luggage than I could handle. This kind official promised us assistance, priority boarding and a cabin as soon as the ship started to accept passengers.

Baby Joanne did not let him forget his promise as she was lacking sleep, was hungry and roaring at such a pitch, that everyone kept well out of earshot to get some relief from the howling noise from our inconsolable baby.

The official kept his word, he found us a cabin and helped with the luggage, apologising profusely for all of the inconvenience that had been caused. We ate in the cafeteria on board and obtained hot water for a much needed bottle for Joanne even managing to get some rest in preparation for a long train journey that still awaited us from Rosslare to Mallow, which was not something that we looked forward to with any enthusiasm.

We managed to contact the ever-reliable Willy Leary, the grocer, and he had arranged for someone to pick us up from Mallow Station, which was akin to the relief of Mafeking. After a marathon journey the saga was yet to deteriorate further. Due to a riding accident, their cousin, Danny Healy, had been rushed to Mallow Hospital with a head injury, after falling from a horse only a few days before Nora's impending wedding.

All of the wedding party including Kathleen Mulcahy, Dennis's intended, were sitting down to breakfast on the 30th July 1970, the day of the wedding, when a black car pulled into the yard, carrying Danny's two brothers, Jerome and Jackie, who broke the news that Danny had passed away in the early hours of the morning, a shock which resonated throughout a farmhouse that had barely recovered from the loss of their Mother.

Danny Healy was only 37 years of age and a first cousin to Joan and Nora, he left a wife, Josie, and four small children the eldest seven years of age, and a large Hill Farm just a few miles out of Millstreet at Keim on the Macroom Road and another family grieving at the loss of a husband and father.

It was hastily decided that the wedding had to go ahead in St. Patrick's Church and the reception at Coolcower House in Macroom all as planned, but the dancing and music would be cancelled out of respect to their cousin. The honeymoon was also delayed until after the funeral. Our return journey back to England, while filled with sorrow, was as uneventful as it was arduous, by train and ferry back to collect our car at the ferry port and the long drive back to our home in Streetly.

It had been two very difficult weeks, but our little Grainger family was counting its blessings. We had each other and another baby to look forward to, that duly arrived only a few days late, on the 30th September 1970. A second healthy girl, Michelle Bernadette, entered the world by normal delivery in Queen Elizabeth Hospital. She was a bonny little girl and a joy and delight to her Mum and Dad. However, Joanne only fourteen months old was not entirely happy with this new intruder, and all the attention the newborn was receiving meant she demanded my attention, especially while Michelle was being breast-fed. Further excitement was to follow with the arrival of Paddy and Kathleen who were to stand as Godparents to Michelle, for the baptism at St. Anne's Church with Fr. O'Healy performing the ceremony.

My Mother and Father were equally delighted at the addition of another grandchild, but disappointed at their exclusion from the Godparenting role, due to the promises made at the baptismal ceremony by the Godparents. These strict rules did not enhance their long term aversion to the Catholic Church.

Soon after the Christening, my mother started to experience blackouts and faints, which later led to a stroke. Joan would arrive most days with the two babies and administer her nursing skills, helping Mum with her mobility and household chores. Connie, who was still living at home, also telephoned home every working day to ensure that her mother was up and about. Sadly, less than two months after Michelle's birth, on the 26th November, Connie telephoned home without response and after several attempts, she telephoned me at work expressing her concern. I tried to telephone and also couldn't get a reply and I raced home to find my mother dead in the armchair in the living room. After pulling myself together from the shock and a flood of tears, I telephoned for the doctor knowing that nothing could be done and broke the shattering news to Joan and Connie, advising her to get a taxi home.

By the time Connie arrived home, the doctor had confirmed that there would have to be a post mortem and I left Joan and Connie together and drove to Dad's work place trying to find the words to break the news in person. The coroner's officials collected Mum's remains while the grieving family stood by in silent shock. The funeral had to be delayed, awaiting the issue of the death certificate by the coroner.

Her death was later confirmed as arterial sclerosis and her wish that she should be cremated was adhered to, the ceremony would take place at Perry Barr Crematorium. This was one of the few events that brought the extended Grainger and Bowdler families together. My Dad had lost the bedrock of his life, his wife and partner of 34 years and I had lost one of the great inspirations of my life, a mother that had an unswerving faith in me, when I was the most hopeless of cases at school and always made me believe in myself, had gone from my life, but had left a lasting impression on me. My inheritance was the ambition and determination to succeed, now for her, as much as for my family.

My father was like a lost soul, he depended on his wife to arrange everything, he had always handed his wage packet to her every week unopened, she ran the family budget, paid the rent and the bills, booked the holidays and arranged their social life. He had devoted his whole existence to his wife and family and he retreated into a shell from which he never totally re-emerged. Connie was heavily involved with Highbury Little Theatre, which together with her work as a legal secretary helped to carry her through this difficult time. I had my work and my own family to support me through my grief.

Christmas 1970 was a very sad time as the Grainger Senior and Junior households gathered together in Hazelwood Road. My mother in her usually organised fashion had all of her Christmas presents bought before her death. The babies were so small that Christmas had little or no meaning. My sister and father minded the children while both Joan and I attended a solemn and thoughtful midnight Mass and the Christmas festivities were shrouded in a very subdued and sombre atmosphere, laced with memories of Christmases gone by.

Returning to the Sheepcote Street factory after the Christmas break, both Warm Air Systems and the manufacturing company were thriving in a booming house-building bonanza. But a trade dispute was to test my dexterity and tenacity. The warm air fitters were all working on a piece work basis and earning very good money, but much wants more and a delegation arrived demanding a wage rise. I agreed to a rise in the day rate, but would not increase the piecework rates, which I believed were more than generous.

A guy called Reg Woods was the leader of the pack, but Terry McIvor then supporting long ginger hair and beard and resembled Jesus, and Billy Gwylliam of Welsh origin which did not help, together with others fitters believed that they had got me over a barrel. I had substantial work on several sites that had to be completed and required these men, or so they thought, to carry out the installations. They gave me an ultimatum, that if a rise in the piecework rates had not been agreed by the following Friday, they would all down tools and seek other employment.

My character had been strengthened and moulded by my National Service training and I would not be blackmailed. I would never let the 'Tail wag the Dog' and I had all of their National Insurance cards stamped up to date and wages made up, with the week in hand included, when they arrived collectively on Friday afternoon. Their position was unchanged, they were leaving on mass. I told them to hand over all of their tools, which belonged to the company and on receipt of the tools, handed them their cards and wage packets. Most of them were gob smacked, but pride, in front of each other would not allow them to back down and my decision was beyond retraction.

All over that weekend, I thought 'Bloody Hell', how would I extract myself from my own unflinching pig headedness, but by Monday morning several of the fitters who had only been driven on by Woods came back, Terry Mc.Ivor included and by using Pat Fitzpatrick and one other sheet metal worker from the factory to replace the ones who did not return, another crisis was overcome and new fitters were recruited without an increase in costs

I must have had some mortar running through my veins, because I planned an extension to the Hazelwood Road property and I drew up a kitchen extension plan, which I submitted to Walsall planners for building permission. After a few modifications, planning was granted and building was soon underway. I called upon all of my early technical school brick laying lessons and did all of the building work single handed, until it came to the plastering and I had to seek a quotation. The best price was £400 and I decided that I could not afford to part with that amount of cash for a day's work so employing some of the techniques that I had watched on sites; I undertook the plastering work with acceptable success.

The completion of the extension coincided with the arrival of spring 1971, which focused our attention on change. The addition of the extra child and more planned, coupled with the growing success of the two companies, we decided to move to a larger house. We wanted to stay in Streetly, but would try to find a house on the posh side of the Chester Road. Number 64 was put up for sale and was quickly sold, for the asking price £5,500. Our house hunting did not take long, as soon as Joan viewed 'Petros' a house name originated by the current owners, Peter and Rosemary in Middleton Road, a house with character and more particularly, a large landscaped garden, which we both liked.

This was the house and home in which Joan wanted her family to grow up I argued in vain that £7,500 for a semi detached house was a lot of money and at the top end of our budget. The five and a half years in Hazelwood Road had made little impact on the existing £3,000 mortgage. But Joan had made up her mind, this was where she wanted to live and her joy and excitement with both the house and the garden lasted all of her life. She would never have been persuaded to leave that house or garden, with its memories of the children growing up and her meticulously nurtured children's paradise, which was an array of paths, trees and bushes all creating a playground for hide and seek and a manicured lawn on which to picnic and push buggies with dolls.

Every year we returned to the farm in Ireland for our summer holidays, I spent most of my time fishing and Joan proudly showing off the children, when visiting relations far and near. Dan was on the point of handing the farm over to Paddy. He felt free and took little persuading to travel with us to England, where he would stay for a couple of months, helping Joan with the garden and on a hot sunny day he would sit under the huge chestnut tree in the shade, smoking his pipe and maybe enjoy a glass of beer. He was a great traveller after Mamie's death, travelling twice to America to meet relatives in San Francisco, seeing the Golden Gate Bridge and the gambling halls in Reno Nevada.

Christmas 1971 was a much happier occasion, the move completed and we were ensconced in Middleton Road Joanne was very excited about Santa, though she was not at all sure who he was, but he brought nice presents anyway. Michelle was walking, but could not understand all this excitement. Connie and Dad stayed with us for a few days over the festive season and showered the children with treats and presents.

Dad was about to retire from work immediately before the Christmas break as his 65th birthday fell on the 2nd January I questioned him 'What will you do to pass the time? he replied 'Nothing, I've worked hard all of my life and I'm due a rest'. He did play bowls at the Barn Social Club and I would buy him a season ticket for Warwickshire Cricket Club each year, but his ambition to enjoy his rest was maintained.

He regularly called to see us and his little treasures most Sundays, bringing sweets for the girls and usually again on Thursday afternoon, arriving about two o'clock, he would stay for dinner and I would take him home around eight in the evening. Dad's addiction to cigarettes was such that in those six hours, an eight-inch diameter ashtray would be filled with Woodbine cigarette butts.

He smoked seventy Woodbines a day and when questioned, he swore that he enjoyed every one of them and although he enjoyed good health all of his life especially considering that he had a polishing job and 70 fags a day, it did take its toll eventually twelve years later.

Back in Sheepcote Street, J.S. Wright had secured a further phase of 500 houses at Wellingborough and placed orders with the fabrication company for their ductwork requirements. At the same time I heard that Mowlem Construction was negotiating a further Phase of 500 houses with the Development Authority. The first phase had gone well and had been profitable.

I was keen to negotiate a price for the warm air installation on phase two, which was a fixed price contract I pitched the quotation at 5% higher than the previous contract to cover the cost of inflation. Between

October 1971 and February 1973 inflation had not gone above 4%.

Additionally I also saw an opportunity to expand the business further and I employed John Birch who had been the old Paragon Heating's electrical engineer and together we made a bid for the electrical installation work on phase two of the Mowlem project. I knew that I was taking a chance, as I was very much in the hands of John Birch for the costing and supervision of the electrical work. Our quotations were successful for both heating and electrical contracts, which would follow on from the completion of the first phase.

The summer of 1973 brought our usual holiday in Ireland, but this year there was even more excitement with two weddings to look forward to. Kathleen was to marry Sean Reardan a local builder in August. When we arrived all the preparations had been made for a Millstreet wedding with the reception at the Drumhall Hotel in Killarney and a great celebration was enjoyed by all of the family and guests. They were able to appreciate a happy relationship together for many years, adopting two children, John and Donal, before Sean started suffering from chronic depression which eventually led to his death.

Dennis, Joan's brother, was to marry Kathleen Mulcahy in September and it was a great surprise to me that she agreed to marry Dennis, because he was a bit of lad in those days, enjoying many a night out with me, in any number of the local bars. One night I recall drinking with Dennis until 11 o'clock, when he suddenly remembered that he should be seeing Kathleen. We drove over to Kathleen's house at Bweeng near Mallow and Dennis started throwing pebbles at Kathleen's window, asking with a rather slurred Irish accent 'Are you coming out tonight?' Needless to say the response was negative. Another occasion when we were visiting relations at the Eagle's Nest farm, Dennis could not get his car started until Kathleen gave it a push and when it started she had to run after it to get in as Dennis would not risk stopping again in case it stalled. However, they were married in great style at Drumahane Church followed by a reception at the Blarney Park Hotel. In spite of Dennis's unflattering romantic style, they both enjoyed a long and happy relationship with Dennis doting on Kathleen, who did not always enjoy the best of health.

Both weddings were celebrated with big evening celebrations, which was noticeably different from eight years previous when we were married, possibly the greater affluence as farms were expanding with poor land being recovered and as farm machinery became more common adding to the productivity of the farming industry.

A few months after retuning home from the wedding celebrations, I was to learn about another pregnancy and an expected third child. The pregnancy went without a hitch and the 14th July 1974 saw the arrival of a third baby and a third girl, Claire Elizabeth, who followed her sisters into the world via The Queen Elizabeth Maternity Hospital, much to the delight of Joanne, Michelle and a proud Dad. I believed that I was the luckiest man alive, a loving wife, three gorgeous baby girls and two companies providing a comfortable living for us all.

Dan had arrived earlier and helped mind Joanne and Michelle during the confinement and Dennis and Kathleen followed, flying over for the Christening and Dennis did the honours as Claire's Godfather, with Fr. O'Healy receiving an addition to his flock and an extra parishioner at St. Anne's Church.

Claire's arrival made good times better. I was being carried along on a wave of success and was beginning to believe that I had the Midas touch. I secured a large contract from Sheriff Construction for both plumbing and warm air installations at Houghton on the Hill and another large contract at Coventry, but most of the company's expansion was coming through areas where I had little expertise. I was overstretching and was becoming too dependent on others for their electrical and plumbing knowledge and skills, particularly electrical, drainage and lead work.

All of these factors conspired together to turn profits into losses and before the situation could be recovered there was a dramatic change in the economy and in particular the rising rate of inflation. The fixed price contracts based on 5% inflation were looking very unhealthy, when in January 1975 inflation reached 12% but the bulk of my turnover was in fixed price contracts and could not be renegotiated.

I was showing signs of concern as I travelled home with Joan and three small children by car and ferry to Cloughoula for Christmas 1974, after we heard that Dan had been taken into hospital with suspected stomach cancer. When we arrived in Cloughoula we were told that everything was fine and that it had been caught in time. We all enjoyed a subdued Christmas only brightened by the excited children anticipating Santa's arrival, amid tearing off wrapping from presents from many aunts and uncles. Dan came out of hospital before our worried family returned home, but Dan was obviously a very sick man. I did not convey the depth of my business problems to Joan, because of her anxiety about her father's health, but she had a second sense where I was concerned and knew all was not well. This was probably one of the best examples of our unique relationship, that we were both able to empathise with each other without the forensic detail being discussed.

CHAPTER TEN

Ambitions Collapse

My entrepreneurial skills and Midas touch were rapidly losing their shine. The first three months of 1975 were disastrous for us all. As January came to a close Joan's father had been re-admitted to the Regional Hospital in Cork city and the cancer was now diagnosed as terminal. I drove Joan and our three girls back to Ireland for an indefinite stay for Joan to nurse Dan. I had to return immediately. The warm air contracting business was also in terminal decline, but I commuted each weekend via Swansea Cork ferries which had been recently introduced and was a Godsend, when compared with the B&I line on which we had earlier travelled from Fishguard to Rosslare.

Every weekend I commuted back to Joan and the girls, leaving the car at Swansea ferry port on Friday evening, catching the 8.45pm ferry to Cork, returning on the Sunday 8.45pm ferry from Cork, arriving 6am Monday morning in Swansea where I collected my car to drive back to the ever increasing cloud that hung over the Sheepcote Street factory. Air travel at this time was very expensive, an expense that I could ill afford at that time, with Aer Lingus having a monopoly on the

Birmingham - Cork route, which coupled with flight times, ruled out this method of commuting and the weekly haul across the Irish Sea was the best support that I could provide for Joan.

The contracting company was suffering with acute cash flow problems, caused by overtrading and we received a writ from Sankey's, a big builders merchant for a sum of money, which could not be paid and to avoid judgment being taken, we agreed an instalment payment plan to meet the debt, but when we were unable to make a payment, the bailiff arrived putting stickers or distrait notices on desks and assets that could be sold. This was the pressure that I was under between my weekend trips to Ireland, throughout February and March, while seeing Joan's despair with the deterioration in her father's health.

Paragon Warm Air Systems Limited, the contracting company could not continue trading for much longer, as inflation rose each month, the losses increased and the bailiff's visits were becoming more frequent. The company had an overdraft facility at the bank of £25,000, which was jointly and severally guaranteed by all of the directors of the company. The Mowlem contract alone was producing a cash flow of between £26,000 and £30,000 each month. I called a meeting and suggested for all of our well-being that as soon as the Mowlem cheque cleared the bank, a liquidator should be appointed. The two Johns resisted saying that I was being hasty, but I argued that leaving it another month was not in the interests of the creditors and that we were taking a big risk, if for any reason a further big Mowlem cheque failed to arrive. We agreed to give it one more month and by mid February when the Mowlem cheque cleared, a liquidator was appointed, with the bank deficit standing at £1,100 and Midland Metal Fabrications Ltd. a creditor with a debt of £300.

Within days of the liquidator taking control, he issued redundancy notices to all of the staff and the fitters with immediate effect. These redundancies included John Birch, Terry McIvor and Ron Foster who were all close friends. There was no advantage to the creditors in completing projects due to the inflationary price increases in equipment costs that could not be recovered by sales. The inflation rate had dropped from its peak of 15%, but the average monthly rate was still in excess of 10%. Any outstanding retention funds from previous contracts would be slow or impossible to recover. I worked with the accountants and liquidator to produce a statement of affairs to present to a creditors meeting, which after statutory notices were published in the press, was arranged for 12th April 1975 at 11.00am. The Midas touch had been a figment of my imagination.

The pain and anguish that Dan was suffering finally came to an end when he passed away late on 8th April, his wake was held at the farm, where he had lived and worked all his life and the Requiem Mass was arranged for 12th April 1975 at 11.00am. At exactly the same time that I was facing angry creditors, without any support from my fellow directors, Joan was burying her father without any support from me. Even in retrospect and 35 years on from this date and this hour it was one of the three lowest points in my life.

I hurried from the creditor's meeting, speeding down the motorway to Swansea to get the night ferry and Dennis, Joan's brother, with whom I had shared great friendship and camaraderie, met me in Cork. But

Dennis's disappointment and betrayal that I had missed his father's funeral was apparent, although little was said either by me by way of explanation or Dennis in recrimination. It was left for the passage of time to reveal the cause and effect and the wounds to be healed. Joan being the eldest, while grieving with her own loss, became the mother figure and stayed over for another week, with the family all helping to comfort each other, but I had to return home to start picking up the pieces. I completed the odyssey in this saga the following weekend taking the car on the ferry to bring Joan and the children back home to a cold and desolate house.

The decline in our family fortunes had been rapid and dramatic, but for Joan and the children the despair at their future prospects was overshadowed by the loss of her father.

After returning to Middleton Road and a broken night's sleep, Joan, with despair in her eyes, standing in the kitchen said, 'What are we going to do?'

'We've not got much choice, we've got to pick ourselves up, dust ourselves down and start all over again.' I replied, more in hope than in expectation. I was also reminded of one of my father's stock phrases. Dad had always been a very good card player, particularly Whist and my father had said Son, any fool can play a good hand of cards, but it takes a good man to play a bad hand.

All was not totally lost and with my father's quotation ringing in my ears, and with the deck stacked heavily against me, I set about the battle to save Midland Metal Fabrications Ltd., the manufacturing company, knowing it would be a gargantuan uphill climb. The bank was still owed £1,100 pounds, which had been personally guaranteed and our biggest customer, Paragon, had been liquidated, leaving a small but irrecoverable debt. Joan insisted on returning to work, but with three small children the eldest only six, it was not practical even if she worked nights.

I was due some statutory redundancy pay from Paragon, which had been introduced by the Government ten years earlier. The redundancy money cleared the bank debt. I negotiated with the landlord to transfer the lease to the surviving company, two of the four sheet metal workers were laid off with a promise they would be reinstated as soon as more work could be found. The machinery were assets which did not have great value, but had been bought by Midland Metal Fabrications Ltd. (MMF) and could not be sold by the liquidator, which left me with some very old and outdated machinery to work with.

In addition, the MMF business was low material cost, high labour and delivery costs, and it was not bound by any fixed prices, all directly opposite to the now defunct contracting company. A major attribute in its favour was that both companies had different suppliers, MMF basically only required a steel supplier, which had not taken a hit with the liquidation. I organised and implemented a piecework system to control labour costs and did the steel buying and delivery of the finished goods myself. No other Paragon Warm Air employees survived the liquidation I was again standing alone and would either rise or fall by my own efforts.

My first priority was to find more sales and work for the surviving company. Ductwork was still being supplied weekly to J.S. Wright at Wellingborough, who always paid their bills on time. I needed to become a super salesman, a job, which I did not relish but needs must. My first early success came after a meeting with the Johnson and Starley representative in Bristol, Roy King, a very helpful salesman with a broad Somerset accent. Johnson and Starley were by now the biggest manufacturer of warm air units, I figured that wherever they sold their heaters, ductwork would be required. Roy suggested that I make an appointment with Phil Sampson the buyer at Drake and Skull in Bristol, a major heating and plumbing contractor in the South West, as they had several large warm air contracts in progress and pending. Additional leads that he gave me were Howard Heating, Austin Heating and Wiltshire Heating in Swindon, who all had numerous warm air and ventilation projects. The work was there to be found and won and I almost wore a groove in the M5 motorway making calls to all possible contacts offering my limited range of products.

I devised a simple selling aid, offering to produce isometric drawings of the ductwork layout and number the parts to help the fitters on site to identify where to install the various components. The Drake and Skull engineers were over the moon with this idea and all of their ductwork orders were quickly on the way to MMF. Drake and Skull also paid their bills on time, which was extremely important, as cash flow would become more and more critical if the business was to grow on a shoestring.

I had employed Pat Fitzpatrick in the capacity of foreman, he was good at his job and I was able to re employ the two guys that had been laid off earlier, Joan was back doing the book keeping, and when production got busy my Dad would forsake some of his well-earned rest to help work in the factory. The first year after the

Paragon crash, the turnover was only £26,000 which was not a lot to buy steel, pay wages and transport costs, and the delivery van was on its last legs, only held together by rust. But I managed to pay the mortgage and feed Joan and the kids.

Cash was still very tight and scarce early in 1976 when Joan told me she was expecting our fourth child, our excitement and delight was a further incentive to find more customers. I travelled to the Manchester area and scoured the yellow pages looking for warm air heating contractors who would let me quote for their ductwork requirements. The Terrian Engineering Company was one of several companies that promised me orders in the Manchester area and now the M6 motorway was a regular route as I built my business connections in the North West.

Our whole operation was very tight, my sheet metal workers were the producers working on piecework rates, the only other overhead in addition to the building costs, was myself I was salesman, driver, I would promise quotations by return and would also work in the factory if production fell behind at any time. Our prices were very competitive and I worked early mornings, late nights and most weekends. My only time off was for anti-natal appointments, minding the children, while Joan was in hospital.

The all too vivid memories of the previous year and monumental climb back was barely off the ground when Kathleen Marie, our fourth daughter was the QE Maternity Hospital's fourth customer from the Grainger family. We were all delighted and excited when on the 24th September the new baby arrived, Kate was born by normal delivery, but Joan had had a difficult time and was very anaemic after the birth. She remained in hospital for ten days after the delivery, which left me doing my best, with the help of my Dad and my sister, to take Joanne to school and mind Michelle and Claire. I was greatly relieved when my beloved midwife returned to take the helm of the family ship, steering it back to its usual tranquillity. Claire, who was only a little over two, stared in wonderment at the new arrival and kept repeating over and over, 'nice baby Mummy.'

The following year the turnover was doubled to £52,000, and again through my South West contact Roy King, who was now a close friend, I was given a lead with a company in Bournemouth who had a large Ministry of Defence contract in Weymouth, mainly naval housing accommodation. After an initial meeting I secured a large order, at a good price, but the logistics were difficult as the ductwork had to be pre-insulated. I would be on the road at 5.30am to deliver to Howard Heating in Swindon first when they opened at 8.00am and then on to a company in Whitchurch, where I had pre-arranged to have the Weymouth ducting sprayed with polyurethane foam insulation, this operation took about two hours. All insulated ductwork was re-loaded on to the van and on again to Weymouth Naval Barracks, before returning home the same day, to be greeted with a kiss and a hug from Joan with all of the children fast asleep with shiny faces after the bath time capers.

I would repeat this routine about every two weeks, but on one occasion the rusting and abused Ford van hit back with a vengeance and when I stopped on the return journey to re-fuel, the van stubbornly refused to start. After much cursing and begging for a tow off the forecourt to jump-start the van and after a long delay,

I was on my way again. Bearing in mind I had been out since 5.30am when I finally reached home at 10.30pm Joan had convinced herself that I had been in an accident. When she heard the front door bell, she was sure it was a policeman bearing bad news and she collapsed into my arms in a flood of tears. What a blessing a mobile phone would have been in those days?

Throughout 1977 the business was growing healthily, a brand new, six foot Edwards Guillotine had been purchased on hire purchase, together with two additional spot welders and a lockforming machine. The unreliable and cantankerous old van had been replaced with a better and more road-worthy second hand van. An office junior was taken on to type invoices, statements and quotations. She also answered the telephone and made tea for the men in the factory, now up to five, who were able to work almost as much overtime as they wanted. I was quite shocked one day when I entered her office to see scantily clad male pin ups adorning the walls of her office and when I commented on the redecoration, she pointed out that the men in the factory had female pin up's, so why couldn't she improve the rather bland décor of her office. This must have been the start of the Women's Lib era, but to get back to more mundane issues, the company was operating without an overdraft and was now in fact in surplus at the bank and the turnover had reached £156,000.

The Bournemouth company had won a large ventilation contract at the Co-op at Wetherby in Yorkshire and asked MMF if we would quote for the supply and installation of the ductwork. I knew that this would cause major logistical problems, because the factory was already flat out, but it was not in my nature to turn work down. I contacted Terry McIvor, a fitter who had previously worked for Paragon, who was now working for himself as a freelance fitter and a price was agreed with Terry to carry out the installation work. The normal everyday manufacturing would be done during the week and at the weekend I would work in the factory, with Pat Fitzpatrick and whoever else would work weekends, to make the ductwork for the Wetherby Co-op.

We had to make enough material at the weekend to keep Terry busy all week carrying out the installation. Everything that had been completed would be packed into the van late Sunday night and I would take the van home and be on my way at 5.30am on Monday morning to ensure that when Terry arrived on site at eight o'clock in his battered Citroen C5, he would have materials to install. This became a normal routine for several weeks before Christmas. The Christmas break brought some relief, when the site closed down for the Christmas holiday, which gave me and my merry men an opportunity to get ahead.

My Christmas holiday this year was confined to Christmas day and Boxing Day with Joan beavering away with the culinary delights while I played with the children and their presents, returning back to my childhood with jigsaw puzzles, Snakes and Ladders and Ludo.

The Wetherby contract was finally brought to its conclusion one Sunday early in February, when my idea of an early birthday present for Joan was a trip to the Co-op with the children, travelling by car to the Yorkshire site, encountering snow and blizzard conditions on the way to take the grilles and vents which were bought in components and the last elements to be fitted.

On completion of the Co-op project, Terry didn't have anything else lined up and I asked him if he would join MMF to work for me in the factory, driving, or on site fitting as situations arose. He agreed and a long lasting friendship and business relationship was forged. It was surprising in many ways that it did survive, because Terry had only been back a few months when I went on one of my many trips to Ireland and on my journey up to the Hollyhead ferry, I passed Terry standing by a broken down van on the M6 motorway. I could not delay as I had a ferry to catch, so I sailed by, leaving Terry stranded, but I had every confidence that he would sort himself and the company while I was away. This situation was a source of humour for many future years.

It was at this time, just after Claire had started school at St. Anne's that I became a member of the Parent Teacher Association (PTA), helping to organise social events and raising money for school funds. The PTA was a very energetic committee of seven chaired, by Jim Ward, the headmaster a small jovial man with a terrier type temperament, a teacher representative, which for most of my tenure was Viki Dickins. I became treasurer and a permanent member, Rob Harrison and four other parents, who would only serve for a two year term of office, as Jim was keen to bring in new people and fresh ideas to stimulate enthusiasm to the working committee.

Jim would list items, which he believed would benefit the school and the PTA would try to raise sufficient funds, much as most PTAs work today. But on the tenth anniversary of the school's opening, an extra effort would be made. A costly item appeared on the list, video recording equipment and plans were formulated for a mega summer fete followed by an evening's grand dance in the school hall.

The highlight of the day was to be an 'It's a Knockout' competition, which was a popular television programme at the time. Teams were sorted out and various amusing relay races organised. One memorable race entailed one person sitting in a wheelbarrow holding a bucket of water on a tray high above their head, while being wheeled by another team member to the finishing line, to discharge the remaining water into a vessel to be measured. Of course, everyone taking part got soaked to the amusement of the onlookers.

All manner of stalls, plants, cakes, white elephant stalls, swing boats, football-shooting competitions, even pony rides were all fund raisers. The day was a scorcher and the ice scream sellers had to replenish stocks from a nearby supermarket.

A parent had provided a caravan, which would act as a command post and although I was counting pennies and other coinage well after everyone had left, it was impossible to calculate the success of our efforts, the target was £1200 but my initial forecast was only up to about £800 when I left to prepare for the dance. No one had considered the volume and weight of coinage that would be generated, which took two days to count and bag for the bank.

The dance in the evening was also oversubscribed, the magistrate had asked for guarantees that the fire certificate for 140 would not be exceeded when granting the license as the PTA was running its own bar. I had attended the Aldridge and District Magistrate's Court to obtain the license a few weeks before. The evening was a great success and finally when all of the money had been counted and two huge bags of coins deposited in the bank, the target of £1200 had been exceeded.

Another highlight of the year was the school ramble, usually held on a Sunday in flaming June, which did not obey the flaming rule every year, but it was always organised with great attention to detail by Peter Dickens, Viki's husband, to cater for a wide age range of hikers, This was not about fund raising, but was very popular with parents and families as an inexpensive day out. It was an event that we all enjoyed every year, with one exception when I had to carry Joanne on my shoulders most of the six miles when she became ill and was diagnosed with scarlatina by the doctor on Monday morning.

I remained as treasurer for seven years, before I finally found a successor and on leaving I was presented with a carriage clock with an inscription, acknowledging my contribution to the school that all four of our daughters would attend. I still treasure that carriage clock with fond memories of happy times and it still holds a place of prominence in my house.

During my tenure as PTA treasurer, I also served for three years as a School Governor after being approached by Fr. O'Healy the Parish Priest to become a Diocesan representative on the Board of Governors, however I found this a thankless task, dealing with LEA officials that were more interested in procedure than getting things done although through my endeavours and determination, St. Anne's was one of the first schools to have a Nursery Unit added.

The parking at the entrance to the school became another battleground for me when the clinic next door posted No Parking Notices notice with a caveat that it was health centre property and the parking was reserved for their use only. My longevity residing in Streetly had given me the knowledge that the clinic, school and library had all been built under the jurisdiction of Aldridge and Brownhills District Council, which later gave way to Walsall Metropolitan Borough Council and I doubted if the records of ownership had ever been transferred. I wrote to the Town Clerk asking for proof of ownership of the land and when I did not receive a reply, I enlisted the help of local councillors. They helped to arrange a meeting with an official from the Town Clerk's office, who had to admit that ownership of this piece of land could not be fully established as it was all part of the original site access when the school was built, and as a result the No Parking signs were removed and parents were allowed to park unhindered.

These were only small diversions from work as I started looking for further ways to expand the business, with associated products that could be sold to the same customer base. I started to focus on the manufacture of aluminium grilles and diffusers and looked at the products that were already in the market. I took them apart and looked at ways of modifying and improving them. After spending time on some costing, I believed that the set up costs were affordable. I set about drawing my own extrusion profiles. Seven were required to cover the initial range. The extrusion manufacturer Aalco Ltd. only required a nominal charge of £70 per tool for the extrusion, provided that they were given an order for £500 per extrusion. The seven extrusions would cost £4,000 for the initial order.

Terry's brother Peter had his own tool making business, Pejo Engineering, and he would make the press tools required for between £200 and £300 each and eight would be required so £2,500 would cover this cost. In addition, two aluminium crop saws would cost a further £400 each. I calculated that for an investment of less than £10,000, I could be up and running with components that until now I had bought in. A new company was formed, Graire Distribution Ltd., the name originated by combining Grainger and air together. The first grilles were produced and the quality established before photographs were taken and a brochure sent to press for marketing and sizing this new range of products, which included weather louvers, diffusers and egg crate grilles.

A mezzanine floor was constructed over the existing office to provide a new office, which was later described as a tree house, but it provided extra space, at little extra cost for the aluminium grilles to be made. I made all of the initial orders myself to establish manufacturing and wastage costs, before training two young operatives to carry out what was a fairly basic process.

It was at this time that 16 year old Michael Rabbit joined the company. He left school and was going from place to place asking for a job He met me in the entrance and I was so impressed with this lad's determination to get a job, that I asked Michael 'Do you want to start straight away?', his response was could he start tomorrow, because he wanted to go home and tell his Mum that he had got a job. Michael Rabbit was still doing sterling work for MMF thirty years later.

In the following year, June 1979, on one of the rare half terms that I spent with the children, I took Joanne then ten and Michelle nearly nine, to the Ironbridge Museum for the day. Joan stayed home minding the smaller children. During the outing, which we were all enjoying, I noticed that Joanne was very lethargic and lacking in energy and we had lunch out in a pub, which was a novelty for the girls. On our return, I mentioned to Joan that I thought Joanne was unusually quiet and passive. Alarm bells started ringing when Joan confirmed that Joanne had been drinking more liquid than usual and having trained as a nurse Joan could recognise the symptoms and could guess the diagnosis.

We made an urgent appointment with the doctor next day and he confirmed that Joanne's sugar blood count was very high and she would have to be admitted to hospital, our worst thoughts were confirmed. Joanne was type one diabetic. Joan was very distressed and upset as she felt that she was responsible, because of the history of diabetes on her side of the family.

It was now my turn to console Joan. I reminded her of my own Grandmother's diabetes, which may also have contributed to the genealogical makeup. Joanne was admitted to Harvey Ward at Good Hope Hospital to be stabilised and taught how to inject insulin, practising on an orange with water in the syringe. She was also taught how to test her own blood sugar levels and all about carbohydrate rations. She had to draw up a glass syringe with insulin and inject herself before she left hospital. She was also taught about sterilising the glass syringes and needles by boiling them. Only a few years later everything became disposable, dispensing with the need for sterilisation.

Joan's nursing experience was invaluable and she coped very efficiently with the medical and practical side of Joanne's condition, but Joanne was at a rebellious age and unwilling to change her diet and withdrawal from sweet foods, which made her a difficult diabetic, who was racing towards puberty. Psychologically, it was an upsetting time and affected all of the family with sympathy for Joanne when we had to be tough, for her own welfare, with many trips back to Miss Mansfield, the Consultant Paediatrician. This medical set back also coincided with Joanne leaving St. Anne's Primary School in July to start Blackwood Middle School in September and advising the teaching staff of the signs to watch out for if Joanne's blood sugar levels became unstable.

CHAPTER ELEVEN

Flues and Chimneys

Christmas 1979 was to be special, as it was to encompass another wedding celebration. Joan's brother Donie, was to marry Mary and their marriage had been arranged for New Year's Day. There was a certain amount of trepidation about our journey to Ireland with past experiences in mind, but all went without a hitch. The Nuptial Mass would take place in St Patrick's Church, followed by a snowy drive to the Creedon's Hotel reception at Inchegeela, with much joy at the festive and nuptial celebrations. Following the festivities we returned home by ferry to await the arrival of the newly weds who were flying to England to spend their honeymoon with us.

We all enjoyed their company, and they were able to enjoy the big city entertainment that was not as accessible when living in Millstreet. I took them to see a live wrestling match, which is so common on television today. Their return home was delayed by a substantial fall of snow, which affected their flight after a light aircraft crashed on the runway closing the airport for two days.

With the Christmas holiday over it was back to work and I started looking for new ways to expand the business. My first association with prefabricated flue systems was the addition of Rite Vent flues to our range of products. I worked on the basis that, wherever a warm air unit was installed it would require a flue system in addition to the ductwork and grilles that were now being manufactured by MMF as standard products. I had only taken into stock the 4" 'B' Vent range, manufactured by Rite Vent in Washington, County Durham. This product was suitable for most warm air heaters and was only a small stock range of components, but would add to our sales and by chance lead the company in a new direction. These types of flue systems were now getting well established, having taken over from the asbestos cement flues, which the defunct Paragon Company had fitted.

The main prefabricated flue manufacturers needed stockists and distributors. They were relying on builder's merchants to distribute their products, but the merchants only wanted to stock a narrow range of the fast moving items, similar to what MMF were doing with the 'B' vent range. The two main manufacturers, Rite Vent and Selkirk, which between them held 90% of the pre-fabricated flue market in the UK, were both looking to establish a specialist stockist network, to stock and distribute their complete range of products. The Specialist Flue Company based at Sudbury in Suffolk was the first specialist stockist and had become spectacularly successful, both for themselves and the manufacturers.

John Hornby, the local Rite Vent representative approached me, suggesting a move by MMF in the direction of becoming a specialist distributor would lead to success. John was aware that the Rite Vent national sales manager, Graham Sandall, was considering setting up his own operation in Birmingham and did not believe that would be in his best interests. He would have liked to start his own company, but did not have sufficient resources, so as an alternative he set up a pub lunch meeting with me, and I was quickly convinced that between us, we could become very successful. I had the space and limited funds to carry the stock, and John was a super salesman, who had all of the contacts throughout the Midlands. He would not only sell a lot of flue systems, but would also boost my own sheet metal sales to a similar customer base. Possibly a match made in Heaven, time would tell if we gave it a chance.

It had not taken very much to convince me, as I was already concerned that the housing boom was in decline and domestic warm air systems were being over taken by pipe work and radiator installations. I had already purchased the six-foot guillotine in preparation to make commercial ductwork and this new idea of different product lines fitted in very well with my diversification thinking.

But it was still a big step for me to take, over stretching in previous years weighed heavily on my mind. I had to improve on John's current salary and provide him with a brand new Ford Cortina Estate car. However, the genes inherited from my mother were still part of my gambling instincts and as a result, John Hornby left Rite Vent with their blessing, knowing that he intended to mastermind a specialist flue distributor in the Midlands and would help to promote and distribute their products.

Within days of him joining MMF, a meeting was set up with the Rite Vent sales director and much to my amazement; he made an offer to put £50,000 worth of consignment stock into MMF, which would only be paid for when sold. John negotiated new terms and bigger discounts to ensure that we were competitive. As soon as this deal had been done, John advised me that to do the job properly, we needed to get the biggest manufacturer, Selkirk on board, as they were much stronger on commercial flue systems, and in addition, they had a bigger market share.

John knew the local Selkirk representative Bob Pearson from meetings at exhibitions and as competitors. He approached Bob with a view to selling Selkirk products alongside the Rite Vent range. Bob, who was a diminutive, fairly dour and unimaginative character, was very reluctant and not at all enthusiastic. But when he reported back to his sales director, the response was immediate.

I received an urgent invitation to bring John to Barnstaple in North Devon to develop the proposal. The following Sunday Bob Pearson, who lived in Sutton Coldfield, collected both of us after lunch and took us to the exclusive Poi'ers Hotel in Barnstaple, to meet Ken Evans, the Selkirk sales director. In a private dining room and over a very well presented, pleasant and imaginative cold buffet dinner, we started to build a better understanding of each other and our current position. We went on to discuss our visions for the future distribution of flue products. John's enthusiasm for selling was music to Ken Evan's ears, like an orchestra being conducted by a maestro.

Ken was desperately keen to expand his specialist distribution network. He had Specialist Flue in Suffolk, Flue Stox in Manchester, Whiteside Chimneys in Liverpool and Docherty's in Reading. The last thing that Selkirk wanted was to have his competitor, Rite Vent, with an exclusive specialist distributor in the Midlands. Throughout the discussions over dinner, Bob Pearson the

Midland representative constantly put objections forward, only to be jumped on by his boss.

Incidentally, this was the first night that I had stayed away overnight from Joan and my little cherubs on business, since the date of our marriage fourteen years previous.

The following morning after an early breakfast, Bob had been instructed in no uncertain terms to change his attitude and drive his prospective customers to his office for nine o'clock. Ken welcomed us again and outlined his proposals for the day. We were first given a tour of the modern, efficient Barnstaple factory, particularly impressive to John, who was comparing it with the Rite Vent setup. After a short coffee break, we had a brief meeting with John Botton the chief executive and Brian Greenslade the financial controller, who by then, would have established that MMF were a small, but rapidly growing company. Then back to lunch in the combined office and factory canteen. After lunch we were to meet in Ken's office to try to strike a deal.

I was quite overwhelmed when Selkirk not only proposed to match Rite Vents offer of £50,000 worth of consignment stock, but with better terms and discounts than their competitor. A small hiccup occurred over my need to manufacture my own single wall stainless steel flue, but a compromise was agreed that MMF would not switch any Selkirk customers to their own manufactured product. With handshakes all round, the meeting broke up with us all agreeing that both companies could look forward to a mutually successful business relationship together.

On our return to Birmingham, Bob Pearson would put a £50,000 order together of the products that he wanted stocked in Birmingham and he would control the stock levels and only replacement stock orders would be paid for.

As John Hornby had predicted, everything on the flue side was moving at the speed of sound, I drew up a business plan and cash flow forecast, with the £100,000 injection of stock from my two main suppliers and made an appointment with Lloyds Bank, with whom I had always banked. I asked for and with little difficulty, was able to agree a £60,000 borrowing facility. In 1979/80 the availability of funding had eased greatly, so much better than it had been ten years previous, when I was looking for a mortgage, but to put the figure into perspective, the maximum jackpot on the football pools at that time was £75,000, which was then considered to be a fortune.

One other turn of events had worked in our favour. The factory unit opposite was empty and had been unoccupied for several months after Haniaway Fabrications had gone into liquidation. I agreed a rent free period of three months with the landlord and gained permission to erect two mezzanine floors on the left and right sides of the long rectangular building, with clear access down the centre aisle. Everyone mucked in, including Terry's father, for two weekends to get these mezzanine floors erected and ready to receive the big stock orders as they arrived.

Selkirk Products were stored on the right, Rite Vent products on the left, all products right across both ranges up to 12" diameter were being stocked by a company, which both technically and logistically was now way ahead of anything else in the Midlands. We purchased a new Luton van on hire purchase and employed a second driver. John Hornby, who had earlier been described as a super salesman, more than matched this description and together with Bob Pearson the Selkirk representative, who was now very enthusiastic and could see that by helping to drive MMF forward he was increasing his own sales figures and meeting his sales targets. In addition, the local Rite Vent salesman also directed most of his flue sales through MMF for the same reasons.

One other major bonus at this time that was now working to my advantage was the very thing that had contributed to my downfall earlier. Throughout 1979 inflation was running at 10% rising to 14% in 1980. This had a twofold advantage, firstly on the value of the consignment stock which was standing in the books as a creditor of £100,000. The increase in inflation over two years could either be viewed as now being worth £125,000 or on the other hand, the £100,000 debt, only having an equivalent cost value of £75,000, so which ever way it was viewed, it was good news.

I was overjoyed with the way the factoring element of the company was stacking up. The fiscal changes were having a very positive impact in so much that both of my two main supplies were having at least two price increases each year. It was rumoured that John Botton of Selkirk and John Garrod of Rite Vent colluded on these price changes, but whether this was the case or not, they would give MMF the opportunity to place large orders at pre-price increase cost and MMF would then sell at the increased price as soon as the increase was publicly announced, thereby increasing MMF's profitability further. Some may think that I was profiteering, but they would not have thought that a few years before, when it was having an opposite effect on me.

Selkirk was an American owned company and they organised a spectacular promotion to woo their specialist stockists, to which Joan and I were invited. The occasion was Selkirk's 25th year celebrations. We returned from Ireland a few days early and it was arranged that Granddad and Connie would mind the children for the weekend, and we travelled to London by train on Friday afternoon. Selkirk had made bookings into the luxury London Bridge Hotel and an exciting programme for the weekend was awaiting us in our room.

The first item on the itinerary was to meet in the bar for cocktails at six o'clock, which gave us an opportunity to meet some of our competitors from other parts of the country for the first time. Then a coach would take us to a nightclub for a mediaeval banquet. Ken Evans, Selkirk's sales director became King Henry the Eighth for the evening, this was well typecast as he had the correct stature, with the figure of a rugby front row forward and beard all adding to the authenticity of the part. Saturday morning and afternoon was left free for browsing the London shops. We went to Harrods just for a mooch around and were staggered to see a rack of fur coats with price tags ranging between £4,000 and £10,000, something that would not have been found in Brum at that time.

In the evening, we were to meet again for pre-dinner drinks; then would be taken the short distance to a paddle steamer moored on the Thames for a champagne reception, followed by dinner, while cruising up the Thames. At nine thirty, we were asked to go on deck to watch a pre-arranged galaxy of fireworks on the banks of the river, which concluded with a grand finale displaying 'Happy 25th Birthday Selkirk' in fireworks.

Following the firework display, everyone was given chips to play Roulette on the lower deck. The top three couples that returned with the most chips were given prizes. Joan and I won a Fortnum and Mason Hamper for third prize, which contained wine, caviar, chocolate liqueurs and many other exotic goodies. I returned to the hotel very happy and more than a little tipsy, well shepherded by Joan, who never drank alcohol. We returned home by train, after a late breakfast on Sunday, to eagerly awaiting children, who were not used to Mum being away from home.

This was to be Ken Evans' swansong, as he was to leave Selkirk after a dispute with John Botton. It was rumoured that John was unhappy about suggestions of even the possibility of an alliance of the specialist distributors. John was very happy with and generous to his customers as individuals, but would not have tolerated a union of like-minded people, who might conspire together. Ken went on to become a regional director of Wolseley Hughes plc.

Ken's successor was Ron Buttery. An entirely different character, Ron was very laid back and every word would be delivered slowly, with great thought to its consequences, before it was uttered in a droll manner, but he had a good sense of humour and a cavalier approach to his customers and looked after them very well. Ron became a great friend to MMF and also to his own sales team, whose bonuses were heavily linked to sales. At the end of each year, when a boost in sales equated to bigger bonuses, Ron would telephone me and offer extra discount for a £100,000 order. Our friendship was increasing by the minute and when I advised Ron that MMF would not be able to pay for this large stock order until it had been turned back into cash, Ron's reply would be 'Don't worry Tom pay us when you can'.

This whole culture was to build whenever a new product was launched, like ceramic flues, Europa, and other new products as they were being promoted, Ron would ask for a stock order to help launch the product, on a pay for it when you can basis. The result of this whole cavalier attitude to sales was twofold. Firstly the value of MMF stock increased rapidly, which gave great comfort to the bank, as their overdraft facility was underwritten by MMF's stock, debtors and fixed assets. The second effect was that MMF's debt to Selkirk was an ever increasing liability, a fact that John Botton was quite comfortable with at that time, as it gave him power over his distributors to control the sale of competitor's products and the bank certainly had no concern for MMF's creditors.

Christmas 1980 was a very happy Christmas, the business was forging ahead, our children were all at an age when Christmas is a very exciting time and we all returned to Ireland for the Christmas holiday. Sean Reardan, Kathleen's husband, obtained a Father Christmas suit and excited the children even more, when his disguised face appeared, tapping at the farm house window dressed up as Santa. These times were very precious to me, due to the business pressures, I spent little time with the children and it had caused me to take them very much for granted. Most of their early development had been managed so efficiently, almost single handed by Joan. Joanne was much more settled and her diabetes had become absorbed into daily life.

Both Christmas and summer holidays were very important to Joan, who was quite isolated in Streetly with all of her family in Ireland and little contact with the extended Grainger and Bowdler families. The holidays gave her the opportunity to renew friendships with old school friends, family and relations far and near.

Throughout the previous failure and now the whirlwind success, Joan was my rock, totally dependant, never complaining, always encouraging. She was never fazed by the earlier failure and not greatly excited about the current success. Joan had a nice home and garden, four beautiful small daughters and she knew that in spite of my fanatical dedication to work, that I loved her deeply and was doing everything I could for the future well-being of our family. She was playing her part in helping to keep me stress free, always a hot meal waiting whatever time I arrived home and her concentration on the children's education and development all helped to play an important part in creating a loving and secure family environment.

Returning after the Christmas break my role had to change dramatically, from a hands on, do a bit of everything, to an administration and management role. The computer age was dawning and we purchased a Commodore 64 computer with an accounting and stock control software package included. I spent a great deal of time inputting stock codes and customer and supplier details, but it was all work, which I could do at home, at evenings and weekends. This allowed us to see a little more of each other and gave me some time to connect with the girls and the novelty of bath time and bedtime stories. I was amazed that they would want the same story every night, with no chance of skipping a page, as they knew all the stories so well.

Although the Commodore by modern standards was very basic and came with a very limited package of software, once all the data had been loaded on to the system, it would produce invoices and statements. These modules were also linked to the stock control software, which would do automatic postings to the sales ledger and with manual posting of purchase invoices it was able to produce a trading account and balance sheet. This change was to ensure control over a rapidly expanding company and to ensure that the mistakes that had been made in the old Paragon days were not repeated. The system comprised of two floppy discs, one bearing the programme and the other a data disc, which was updated as transactions were entered, but there were limitations on the capacity of the floppy discs.

Soon after the computer had been activated, another product range was added to the MMF stock list, when I successfully completed negotiations with Brevco and their vitreous enamel products were taken into stock. Again, I produced more cash flow and rolling balance sheet forecasts for more negotiation with the bank to increase the overdraft facility to £100,000 pounds

Sales of flue components which only had to be bought in and sold on rapidly overtook to ductwork and manufacturing sales. The ductwork and flue products complemented each other, but they had two distinct differences. The manufacturing side was high labour, low material costs, and relatively high profit margin, whereas the factoring side had high material, low labour cost and relatively low profit margin, even though it was enhanced by inflationary factors. But between the two sides of the company, the turnover rapidly grew well past the £750,000 mark, with a healthy rise in profits, which we re- invested into more stock and better equipment. I only ever drew the minimum salary that was needed to meet our quite modest needs, as cash retained in the business was crucial to the growth of the company.

The sales of flue components continued to grow and I decided to change the name of the company from Midland Metal Fabrication Ltd. to MMF Flues and Chimneys Ltd., which would better reflect the major activity of the company. The grille company, Grair Distribution Ltd., was so overshadowed by flue sales that it ceased to trade in its own right and the activities were absorbed by the main company. The rapid growth in turnover quickly caused problems with the Commodore computer, due to the dual floppy discs having insufficient capacity, the stock control module kept falling over and it was very restricting, in that it was not a multi user multi tasking machine, equipment which was rapidly becoming available.

I started to search for a more powerful computer package with multi tasking, multi user capabilities, with equipment and software to suit our needs. At this time most suppliers were suggesting that it would require a main-frame computer to perform all of these tasks, but the company CMS, based in Erdington, that had supplied the Commodore advised me about an American Alpha Micro computer that would meet our company's requirements and could be easily expanded as the company grew further. The problem was that the software had been written for this operating system, but had not been tested.

After several delays I gave them a deadline as the computer problem was causing havoc with both the limitation of the computer and so much work that had to be repeated due to system failures caused by insufficient capacity of the floppy discs. Eventually after much huffing and puffing, I was taken to the software house in Southampton, while there I checked through all of my main requirements. Firstly, that the invoicing module could discount by product code and customer simultaneously and secondly that it would provide all of the stock valuation reports that I needed. An additional requirement was that it had to have an integrated wages package that would automatically post to the main ledgers, with the month end procedures, while having a multi user capacity.

By seven o'clock that evening having tested and tried working demonstrations, I was convinced that the software would do everything I needed. Our return home was delayed in Southampton for dinner and after three hours of deep thought travelling up the M5, we stopped at Stencham Services on the motorway and after some further negotiation, I finally signed an order for £12,000 just before midnight, on the promise that the complete system would be delivered and commissioned within two weeks.

It was delivered on time and the arduous task of re-inputting all of the data was underway. I elected to do most of this work myself to ensure that I understood every aspect of the new and more sophisticated package. Both systems would then run in parallel, for two consecutive months, to ensure the validity and accuracy of the Alpha Micro system, before going live on the third month.

John Hornby continued to secure almost every potential flue customer in the West Midlands and ensured that they were trading with MMF, whilst I had made a good contact with the Midland Electricity Board. The MEB had started a small air conditioning contracting division, which was being headed by Clive Taylor and he used MMF for the supply of the ductwork, which would be installed by his own personnel. Within a year, Clive realised how profitable this could be and he left a high salaried job with a good pension to start his own company, Exeway Ltd., taking with him all his key personnel, fitters, electrician and service engineer.

Clive had established good contacts with the many working men's clubs in the Midlands, the first being the Barn Social Club where my father bowled and one by one, picked off the various clubs to change the Smokey Bars and Concert Halls to a better environment. He was very successful and our company gained from all of their ductwork requirements.

A further concept that Exeway developed was an environment of controlled heat and humidity for the growth of mushrooms and secured several contracts from large mushroom producers, all of the projects required ductwork from which we benefited. We also won a large order to manufacture and fit nine stainless steel canopies and ductwork at The Grand Hotel in Birmingham, in a total kitchen refurbishment. These multifarious projects were all helping our company to grow on two fronts.

There was one particular project of interest that could have ended in tears. We were installing an air conditioning plant at Birmingham Museum Art Gallery. We were well into the contract with the knowledge that the fire restrictions were rigid and uncompromising, no welding equipment and strictly no smoking. I was on my way back from the bank in the city centre, when I heard the wailing sounds of many fire engines. In sublime ignorance, I thought there must be a big fire somewhere. But I put it to the back of my mind and decided to call in at the museum, through the back entrance, to see how the installation team was getting on. I took the lift and as I arrived at the required floor, the doors opened automatically and as if orchestrated by a great producer, I was greeted by a very stern looking gallery director and a high ranking fire officer, to be told that my fitters had set fire to the Gallery. Visions flashed through his mind, how far would the £2,000,000 Public Liability Insurance stretch, maybe one painting, or possibly two.

On further investigation, I found that the ductwork was being insulated with the specified materials and adhesive, the adhesive however was highly flammable and the fitter's mate, having a crafty and illicit drag, had thrown his dog end and it had entered the glue pot. The two operatives immediately dealt with the quick flare up, but it had activated the fire alarm, which was directly linked to the central fire station and a major incident procedure had been activated.

CHAPTER TWELVE

Another Step Forward

While Margaret Thatcher was assembling her task force to retake the Falklands Islands after they had been invaded and overrun by the Argentine forces, commanded by General Galtieri, who obviously wanted to increase his territories, I was also giving serious consideration as to how I could increase our area of operation and share of the flue market.

Most of the flue business had been won in the West Midlands by 1982 and I believed that it would be possible to repeat the Birmingham flue model in the East Midlands. My first approach was to contact Fred Fredericks of East Midland Chimney Supplies, based in Nottingham, to see if he would sell out to MMF. I had two meetings with Fred, but his company was making meagre profits and was tied in to an expensive lease with high rates. He rejected out of hand my offer of £25,000, which was based on what I believed it would cost to start a new branch from scratch.

This led me to check out other properties in the area, but high rent and rates led me to extend the search to Mansfield, where I found a vacant transport depot, which was owned by a Mrs. Flowers, the widow of the owner of Flowers Transport, which had closed down on the death of her husband. The property was being offered on a low rent and had a reasonable rateable value. The arched Belfast roof of the warehouse building offered excellent storage facilities and was situated within two miles of the M1 motorway; the premises backed on to the Railway Station in Victoria Road.

Mrs. Flowers welcomed her new tenants as the building had been standing empty for some time and a lease was signed by a newly formed company; MMF Northern Ltd; a wholly owned subsidiary of the parent company. I informed Selkirk and Rite Vent of our expansion plans and asked for their support to help with the stocking of this new depot. Both were delighted with the prospects of an addition to their distributor network and the probability of increasing the level of trade that they were enjoying with MMF. They readily agreed to give additional discounts and extended credit on the stock orders placed. I contacted Lloyds Bank again with a revised business model for the new depot and the overdraft facility was doubled to £200,000. This was secured against the stock which was now in the order of £250,000, debtors in the region of £150,000 and fixed assets in excess of £50,000.

John Hornby agreed to be based at Mansfield and would recruit and train a manager. The best candidate interviewed was Nikki Dever and she was appointed. Nikki was a bright female in her late teens and learned the products quickly and initially was a great asset. A warehouse man and driver were also recruited easily, as unemployment was high in this now defunct mining town. A team of lads from the factory travelled with John for the first few weeks to weld and erect racking to accept the stock when it arrived. We purchased a new van on hire purchase and we had sign written with the MMF Northern logo and telephone numbers. Within weeks we had the depot up and running and John, with help from the Rite Vent representative, Nick Baines, and Selkirk Representative Alan Kirby, was opening new accounts and generating new business. MMF Northern became profitable by the end of its second year.

The Sheepcote Street premises were by now bursting at the seams, our stock levels were continually increasing, we were adding machinery to expand the manufacturing capacity and the limited access was hampering the handling of the larger deliveries arriving daily. The premises were a very inefficient use of manpower and material handling. We started looking for new larger premises close to the existing workplace, to ensure that the precious and loyal staff would also make the move. We found a three bay factory unit less than two miles from Sheepcote Street, with good access, which would overcome many of the problems being experienced with the old premises.

We entered into a three-year lease for the Clement Street property with Cookson's, a publicly quoted metals company, with options to extend the lease beyond three years. The increased rental and rates were an unwelcome addition to the overheads, but I calculated that the savings in manpower hours with the ease of loading and unloading stock would certainly go a long way to offset the overhead increases, as a high volume of materials was now being handled with forty foot containers arriving weekly from Selkirk.

As the move was taking place, the mezzanine floors were dismantled from the old premises and re- erected in Clement Street, providing a total storage and manufacturing capacity of over 12,000 square feet in an impressive building. As soon as everything was in place and MMF signs erected across the frontage, and the stock neatly racked in product order, John suggested a grand opening, by inviting all the Midlands' customers to an evening of food and music. He wanted to make sure that all of the MMF customers had taken note of the move and to give the sales order staff and me an opportunity to meet our valued customers. Selkirk was always keen to give support to anything that would promote their products and Rite Vent was usually also very helpful.

John invited Selkirk, Rite Vent and Brevco to put up promotional stands and in return they would contribute towards the cost of the evening. Their stands were erected in a large office area on the first floor, which would later become the board room, a bar was set up on the trade counter, and John had arranged for caterers to bring in hot and cold buffet type food.

To create a party atmosphere he booked 'White Lightening Disco' a very psychedelic setup with large screens and flashing lights. All of this in a factory warehouse gave a cavern type atmosphere, which would later have had the appearance of an acid party. It was a huge success, very well attended and was to be the foundation for an even bigger promotion at Liberties on the Hagley Road the following year.

This promotion was the first advertising of any note that MMF had undertaken, but I recognised that it was playing its part in establishing MMF as a big player in the flue market, as well as working towards building better and stronger ties with both our suppliers and customers.

Selkirk products were substantially out selling their Rite Vent competitor, even taking into account the high volumes of flexible flue liner being sold, a product not made by Selkirk until many years later. I believed that it was necessary to strengthen our own sales order staff to cope with the level of orders and enquiries being handled and Chris Dolan and Tim Stilgoe were recruited and after a spell in the warehouse, were promoted to the sales office. The Dolan/Stilgoe combination was the best MMF ever had in this role, orders were processed efficiently, transport organised to a very high level of effectiveness and customer satisfaction was running at its peak at this time. Alan Turberville, a sheet metalworker apprentice, had completed his studies and was to play a greater part when the works manager Matt Spooner, left the company at short notice to join a grille manufacturing competitor.

As the company was growing, so were the children, each developing their own personalities, but all had the same holiday wish and wanted to spend every minute of every day of the school holidays in Ireland. We had to have the ferry booked and the Ford Grenada Estate packed up ready to collect the girls, as they broke up for their school holidays to ensure none of the school holidays was wasted, Easter, Whitsun, summer and Christmas. In the case of the summer holiday, I would take them over at the start of the holiday and return to work after a few days, then take my main two weeks' main holiday in the middle and would then return at the end of the holiday for a few days before bringing them back to home and school. My father also travelled with us for summer holidays and enjoyed the life on the farm in Cloughoula and was always made very welcome by the Healy family.

The girls loved the freedom of the farm and the open rolling countryside and were always up early, to help bring the cows down the fields for milking, collecting eggs from the hen house, haymaking, also, picnics by the river at the bottom of the land, playing shop with old tin cans in the yard and hide and seek with Paddy, Joan's eldest brother, all to the orchestration of honking pigs, cooing guinea fowl, clucking hens and the gaggle of turkeys, all things that they only read about at school. This was a complete recipe for an idyllic paradise for small children. I had started playing golf and still enjoyed my fishing usually in the river Finnow or Blackwater, often bringing back Rainbow Trout for supper. Joan would catch up with all of the news from her brothers and sisters and visit all of the aunts, uncles and cousins. In addition, there were trips to Killarney and the seaside, exploring most of Cork and Kerry over the following years. The numerous islands off the Cork and Kerry coastline were big attractions, Bear Island, the cable car at Dursey Island, Sherkin and Clear Islands, the seaside and beaches at Glenbeigh or Rosscarbery, and The Healy Pass were all a myriad of exciting places to be explored.

The accommodation at the farm was becoming more of a problem as Donie and Mary now had children of their own, Dan and Marie, and it was at this time that Joan reminded Paddy and Donie of their father's offer to give a plot of land to Joan if ever she wanted a house at Cloughoula. Donie and Mary were only too happy, as this would alleviate the overcrowding problem at holiday times. The only suitable plot was a half-acre site at the top of the land, where the Healy property met the road. I drew up plans and applied for planning permission. The plans were approved quite quickly as there were very few restrictions at that time and Joan's brother in law, Sean Reardon, agreed to build the bungalow for us. We would bring funds over when coming to Ireland and Sean would build it, whenever his work was slow. It took about two years to build and cost 15,000 punts at that time. We became more and more excited each holiday as we saw our own holiday home taking shape.

Several years after the bungalow was completed, a rift occurred that split the Healy family, fuelled by Joan's sister in law, but it isolated her husband and Joan's youngest brother Donie and to a lesser extent eldest brother Paddy from Joan, Nora and Dennis with Kathleen walking a tightrope between both factions and any family visitors to the Cloughoula Family Farm that had been their family home, became Persona non Grata. The animosity arose out of the failure of their late father Dan to make a will, and a fracture and wounds that were inflicted were never allowed to heal.

The holidays came to an end and noses were back to the grindstone, school for the girls and work for me. The Mansfield branch was well established when John Hornby on his way to the office suffered what turned out to be a mini stroke. John being the man he was, carried on regardless, thinking it was just a very bad headache and somehow drove back again that evening. After booking an urgent doctor's appointment the next morning, he was rushed into Rushall Hospital and the stroke was diagnosed. It was a minor stroke and although not debilitating it was a warning, but John couldn't wait to get out of hospital with his pills and get out selling again, but when I visited John in hospital I urged him to take the doctors advice and slow down, as he would not be able to sell anything if he was prevented from driving.

It was not long before John was back at work, fuelled by the adrenalin that selling gave him and the aphrodisiac of winning new business, and he started by organising another big promotion, this time at Liberties on the Hagley Road.

To help organise the event, David Smirthwaite, who had only recently been appointed national sales manager for Selkirk, invited Joan and I, John and his wife Jean together with Alan Kirby and his wife, John Frazer and his wife all for a night out at Liberties. The meal was ostentatious even by Selkirk standards and the champagne flowed to the extent that when the bill for £1600 was presented David Smirthwaite or 'Smugger' as he was known, realised that he would have trouble in getting this amount through his expenses. He apologetically asked me if I would settle the bill and told Alan Kirby the Selkirk domestic product representative to authorise the supply of flue product, free of charge to more than the value of the cost of the meal. This was not an unusual method of payment as most promotional assistance came in the form of free products.

The Liberties promotion that followed was sponsored by Selkirk and was another huge success. John knew so many customers and contacts within the trade and was buoyed up with his infectious enthusiasm for selling and his customers. The staff from Mansfield came to help look after the many guests and Smugger took more than a paternal interest in Nikki Dever plying her with champagne, which was the catalyst for him to provide similar refreshments for the main organisers. The event was irresistible, most people invited came and everyone had a great night and another promotion had helped to lift our company profile even higher.

But the daily travelling to Mansfield and the memories of his earlier stroke was to take John away from MMF, when he was offered the national sales manager position at his previous employer Rite Vent. He would still be working with MMF, as they were very substantial Rite Vent customers, but his first priority now would be to build a sales team and to promote the Rite Vent range of products only. It would be eleven years before John returned to what I believed was his real home, MMF.

John's decision was a disappointment for me and I believed in the long run that it was a poor career move for John, but the momentum that John had started was unhindered. Paul Bastable was recruited to represent us in the Midlands; he had a dogged determination to earn his keep by generating new business in a wider area. Alan Kirby of Selkirk, together with the John Hornby and Nick Baines combination for Rite Vent, were all bringing new business to us and providing sales leads.

I believed that a really a big hitter was needed to replace John nationally, and I approached Alan Kirby the Midland Area Selkirk representative offering him a salary rise, a car of his choice and position as sales director. Alan agreed to join us and chose a middle of the range Saab car. I also offered Terry a directorship to strengthen his position within the company. These changes helped strengthen the MMF board, but I was still the only real decision maker. Selkirk quickly replaced Alan Kirby with a rising star from their sales office, Dana Davis, whose only claim to fame was his appearance on Blind Date with Cilla Black, however he did not win his date and was never a big winner with Selkirk.

I suffered a further loss when my Dad died of cancer in the middle of 1984. The summer holidays had been booked early in the year to ensure that cabins were available on the ferry, when my father started complaining about back pains and was sent for an X-ray around April time. Within days, Joan and I were called back to the X-ray centre in Corporation Street, to be told that the diagnosis was cancer of the oesophagus and that it was inoperable. This traumatic news was met with silent shock, even taking into account his heavy smoking habit throughout his life, he had rarely visited a doctor and my carefree happy go lucky father had seemed indestructible. We tried to comfort each other, as neither could imagine what life would be like without him.

His condition deteriorated and he was admitted to East Midlands Hospital, now Hartlands, but he kept insisting to the nurses that they had to get him better for his holiday in Ireland in July, but this was destined to be a false hope. I took Joan and the children to Ireland, but returned immediately to be with Dad and to ensure that everything he needed was available. With great sadness I telephoned Joan ten days later and told her that Dad's condition was deteriorating rapidly and to fly back if she wished to see him again before he died. Joan had always been fond of her father in law, who had become so much more over the years and was on the next plane, a small eighteen seat Air Aaron flight, leaving the girls with her brothers and sisters and within a week Dad had passed away, was cremated at Perry Barr Crematorium to rest with Mum, and we returned to the children, to break the sad news that Granddad had gone to Heaven.

My father, although quiet and lacking ambition, had very strong true values of honesty, which were sacrosanct, particularly his family values and this left a lasting impression on me, which were appreciated more and more as I grew older, especially much later when the integrity of government and banks evaporated into oblivion. I still always tried to follow the example that he had set me.

Another holiday over, another Irish holiday blighted with sadness and returning back to sister Connie who now was living alone, but either by good fortune or good planning Connie and her father had taken the opportunity offered by Mrs. Thatcher to buy the council house as sitting tenants at a discount, which gave Connie the security of her home. She had also reached the dizzy heights of Arts Director at The Highbury Little Theatre and had been instrumental in starting the Youth Theatre bringing in a wealth of young talent.

Some normality was restored in Middleton Road by the routine of school and work. Joanne left school that summer and was employed by MMF, starting as a YTS Youth Training Scheme worker on £27 per week, firstly working in the stores to learn the products for the first six weeks, before joining the office staff. My eldest daughter had not been a great academic at school, always calling on her diabetic condition when necessary to escape from things she did not like. I sent Joanne to a private secretarial course, which she had to do on a part time basis.

By Christmas the following year significant changes were taking place at our Mansfield Depot when the manager Nikki left for holiday after collecting her Christmas bonus and did not return in January. She left without giving notice and also left owing me £400 for a loan that I had provided for her to buy a car. I was never repaid and I was very disappointed at the manner in which she left the company.

Chris Dolan agreed to travel from the Birmingham office to Mansfield and filled the breach until Gary Duerden was appointed in February. When Chris returned to the Birmingham sales office, the commercial flue side of the business was also growing with John Frazer, the Selkirk commercial representative and John Hornby now working for Rite Vent bringing in more orders that required installation, in addition to the supply of the material.

I had been doing most of the contracting work myself, but Chris was very keen to take this work on and I was happy enough to give him the opportunity, even though he had had no contracting experience. He had done a great job in the sales office, and had managed the Mansfield branch satisfactorily until Gary Duerden had replaced him; additionally he knew all of the products inside out. But after just a few projects, I knew that this would not work out after a quantity of large diameter and expensive specially enamelled flue was returned from site and had no resalable value, becoming expensive scrap.

I tracked down Ron Foster a name from the old Paragon days. Ron was working as 'small projects' manager for Daly Heating in Coventry and was not very happy that the small projects division always played second fiddle to the main activities of the company and was therefore starved of resources.

He welcomed the chance to take on the commercial installations projects manager with MMF. Unfortunately, this led to the loss of Chris Dolan to EFC, East Midland Flue and Chimney, a competitor in Leicester and although threats were made that Chris would take most of MMF commercial work, I was not in the least worried, because I knew that if he repeated some of the mistakes that he had made with the our company it would certainly be an expensive recruitment for his new employer.

Ron Foster proved to be a charismatic addition to the company growing the contracting section to its peak turnover in excess of £750,000 over the next few years with major prestige contracts at Tate Gallery Liverpool, The Royal Dutch Embassy in London and sixty thousand pounds worth of labour only work for Selkirk at Strangeways Prison to name but a few.

Chris Dolan's departure later attracted an offer to buy MMF, from Chris's employer Copson Heating who also owned EFC. I was interested as I had always had an ambition to retire at fifty years of age, but after preliminary talks, no formal offer was ever made.

However, the interest by Copson Heating influenced my thinking about an exit route. Everything we owned was tied up in the company and maybe it was time to put some cash in our own bank. Our accountants, Starbuck Stone and Co., introduced a guy named John Maccata, who reputedly had many contacts and postured to be a company broker. I engaged him on a retainer and expenses to find a buyer, who was looking to purchase shares in a growth company or to acquire and together expand them both sufficiently, to get quoted on the Aim Market. Over the next two years I had several meetings with a number of companies, but none had any great synergy with MMF and he wasted many days of my time, while he was racking up expenses. However, one meeting with BSS plc, a publicly quoted company, which came to nothing at the time, was to bear fruit many years later.

One of the few pleasant memories that I recall with John, who was a Member of Lords Cricket Club, a membership acquired, he said, because his father had been a High Court Judge, and which John boasted that his father was the last judge to send someone to the gallows. Whether this was true or not, it led to me being invited in to the members' enclosure at Lords and being taken into the Long Room to see a replica of the Ashes trophy. I also saw the opulence of champagne and real tennis being played, a game that I did not know existed and I have never seen a real tennis court from that day to this. But the lack of any cockney accents and the abundance of ex Eton and Harrow pupils supporting the loud red and orange striped Lords' ties were overwhelming and from a different world, never the less, it was an experience that I enjoyed.

The only other notable experience was after I had received an invitation from John to play golf at the exclusive Ashridge Golf Club at the base of the Chiltern Hills and I offered a return game at Great Barr Golf Club, which did not have quite the St. Andrews ring about it. I was only a novice golfer playing off a 22 handicap and managed to beat John conclusively something like five and four, however John was playing off 14, but it still gave me a great deal of satisfaction to defeat this rather superior individual, who drove back to the Chilterns with his tail between his legs, muttering bandit under his breath.

I was still a workaholic, but always tried to dedicate Saturday mornings to my daughters, firstly for many months skating at Solihull Ice Rink, where I, together with the girls, went through the full first six stage courses of Figure Skating and the girls taking part in the Christmas pantomime on ice. Joanne had Hockey Skates and skated regularly with some rather dubious friends at the Silver Blades Rink in Birmingham city centre, and gave Joan and I more than a few grey hairs while waiting to collect her at the bus stop from the last bus home.

Horse riding also became high on the agenda when we bought Lady, a thirteen hand pony mainly to allow Joanne to compete in local Gymkhana's with her friend Lucy. But all of the girls went to Middleton Riding Stables with me in tow for lessons. Neither Claire nor I were very good equestrians and Claire lost confidence and preferred to stay home with Mum after she had a fall from a small grey pony.

The horse riding came to an end when Joanne's interest turned to boyfriends and following a few severe winter months when Joan had to brave the elements to feed Lady, it quickly brought an end to their equestrian ambitions. Skiing came next with a few visits to dry slopes for lessons, but this was also short lived when other priorities mounted as 'O' and 'A' levels were approaching for Michelle and Claire.

Kate's tenth birthday brought surprise and delight when 'Dougal' a light fawn mongrel puppy arrived and literally became a member of the family for over fourteen years. When he first came he was just a small bundle of fluff, chewing everything he could get his teeth in to, but as he grew with the children and later grand children they were mad about him and he was always excited when playing with them. He became a good watchdog, and on many of his trips to Ireland would retrieve golf balls for me when I was pitching golf balls in the large garden at the rear of the bungalow.

However there were a few embarrassing moments, the most memorable was when he arrived back in our garden with a trainer shoe from next door, which had been put out to air and Kate had to return the now, well chewed article to its owner, with an offer to pay for a replacement pair.

Claire's fortunes were also about to take a dramatic change when the diabetic curse struck again, not long after her fourteenth birthday and following a long summer holiday in Ireland, where the symptoms were blindly overlooked in the belief that lightning could not strike twice in the same family. After a week at home and a more normal routine was re-established it became apparent that all was not well and Joan made an appointment for Claire to see the doctor hoping that her worst suspicions were wrong. The diagnosis was not surprising, but another shattering and bitter disappointment and the feelings of guilt returned, brought on by the genetic history.

Claire was admitted to Good Hope Hospital again under the care of Miss Mansfield and she accepted the situation reasonably well. I remember the first hospital visit when treatment was underway that Joan started to cry when she saw Claire with the drips in her arms.

'Mum if you don't cry, I won't,' she said, being well aware that her life would be different from now on, as she had observed the changes in her big sister Joanne's life.

After being discharged from the hospital, she quickly adapted to a new regime of insulin injections, diet and exercise and with a determination to obey all of the rules for a healthy life style.

CHAPTER THIRTEEN

Acquisition Proheat

The growth of the company was relentless with the combined turnover of Midlands and Northern racing past the 1.5million pound mark and profits were increasing annually, when another opportunity presented itself. I learned through the trade grapevine that Proheat Ltd., a company based in Leominster, who specialised mainly in their own vitreous enamel flue products and heavy gauge single wall stainless steel flues, was up for sale. The owner, Mrs. Clegg, a woman of German origin, had suffered with a long illness and wanted to retire. During her illness she employed a married couple Sue and Barry White to manage the business and they had built up substantial turnover, largely with stove shops in Wales and the South West. The vitreous enamel products were being made under a subcontract arrangement with Caradon's in Cardiff, who were eager to pull out of what was a very small sideline for them and the whole situation was getting too much for the ailing Mrs. Clegg.

Barry White, a young man, died suddenly with a brain aneurysm. This left his wife Sue devastated and Mrs. Clegg had to return to the business, only to find to her surprise, that the large turnover was producing very little profit and this combined with poor credit control had brought cash flow problems. She instantly put many customers on a stop list until they paid up. There was an aura of Vee haff Vays of making you pay about her. She also set about re-aligning discounts to increase margins. In effect she lost some low margin business and slow paying customers to try to clean the business up for a sale.

I was greatly attracted to the Proheat company as a possible acquisition, which offered many avenues for expansion. By relocating the company to the Bristol area it would give me distribution in the South West and the combination of both companies' product ranges being sold to Proheat's stove shop and customer base would be a recipe for success. The problems that Mrs. Clegg had with Caradon's reluctance to continue with the manufacturing would also turn to our advantage, as we would move production, in house to Birmingham, providing better control and hopefully lower manufacturing costs.

The logic was undeniable, and although interest rates were high, on the other hand money supply was readily available. Banks were prepared to throw lending at anything that had any chance of succeeding. I offered Mrs. Clegg £150,000 for the business, but it would cost a further £80,000 to buy the plant, equipment and stock from Caradon. In 1987 this was a huge sum of money and due to the nature of it being a combined deal with both Caradon and Proheat it would all have to be funded by the bank.

I took an enormous risk again and went the whole hog with the bank. I had an exceptional ability with figures, probably inherited from my father and now with the aid of spreadsheets I had become expert at producing cash flow and rolling balance sheet forecasts. In fact the spreadsheets allowed me to produce whatever result I was looking for and I could not understand why the bank would place so much store in them. However I secured a £750,000 overdraft facility, which would fund the purchase of the company and provide sufficient surplus cash to increase the stock, together with the removal costs. I engaged David Baxter of Foster, Baxter and Cooksey to carry out the legal work and working late into the evening, the combined deal with Mrs. Clegg's solicitor and Caradon was finally and successfully completed.

Alan Turberville, who had entered into an apprenticeship with MMF several years earlier, was now works manager and he, together with Michael Rabbitt went to the Caradon plant at Cardiff to learn all of the manufacturing techniques and tolerances before the plant was shipped to Birmingham. I had decided to allowed Proheat to stay in Leominster for another two years until the lease expired and to provide some stability while the new company and manufacturing techniques were being integrated into the MMF organisation.

There was also a long learning curve, with the manufacturing and the nuances of stove enamelling to get perfect colour matches. The techniques of manufacture were quickly mastered, but we encountered many difficulties in making the right mix of components in the correct colour and the factory was continually being asked to make small quantities to fulfil back orders. This was totally counter productive and I made the decision to turn to batch production and accept the flak in the short term from unhappy customers, who were not at all pleased at receiving incomplete orders. This decision was not popular with the sales force either, but within three months almost all orders were being fulfilled without back orders and productivity had risen to all time levels.

Caradon continued with the enamelling process for a short period and they provided MMF with the Frit formulae to phase the enamelling away from them, as they really wanted to extricate themselves from these small components, which was only a diversion to their main line, the manufacture and enamelling of pressed steel baths.

Mrs. Clegg stayed on and was offered a sweetener directorship of MMF and I took over as Managing Director of Proheat. She continued to manage Proheat with her existing staff and the company was profitable from day one.

Joanne had not lasted long working for me, she was going through the difficult teenage years and her career was low on her list of priorities, while she was enjoying a good social life and neglecting her diabetic condition. I would always be out of the house and on my way to work early to miss the worst of the traffic and had always insisted that the office and factory should start at the same time, there was no us and them 'office and factory'. I tried to build a team that all worked together. Joanne was never ready for work and was constantly delaying me. I tried to explain with little success that as far as work was concerned, I was not her Dad, but the managing director. I gave her an ultimatum, that if she was not ready to leave the house by seven twenty, I would go without her. The next day I left for work leaving Joanne behind and that evening, we both agreed that it was not working out and that she would seek other employment.

Joanne very quickly learned that her social life and smoking habit needed funding and her poor attainment at school and subsequent lack of qualifications started to change her attitude, as she started job hunting. She was learning the hard way that the good life has to be earned. Her first successful job application was as a care assistant in a very smelly and disgusting Nursing Home on City Road. This really was a wake up call and she quickly found a job nearer home at the Cheshire Homes, still as a care assistant, but this was also short lived. She had been out of work for some time after trying a number of different jobs and was unsuccessful with several job applications, when Julie the receptionist clerk at Proheat became pregnant.

I thought that Joanne had by now learned her lesson and offered her the opportunity to replace Julie at Proheat, but it was on the understanding that she would be working for Mrs. Clegg, a woman with a Germanic sense of discipline. Mrs. Clegg offered her accommodation in her own house until digs could be found in Leominster and as far as Joanne was concerned, this could not happen quickly enough. It was bad enough working with this woman by day without having to socialise at night. Joanne saw Mrs. Clegg as a wicked stepmother, but she would now agree that her new employer was a powerful influence and helped to build a very strong foundation for her future career.

She would travel to Leominster on Sunday evenings and lodge there all of the week, in a town noted for antiques and bookshops and definitely not the hub of the nightlife scene. I would collect her Friday evening returning her to civilisation for a weekend with her family and friends.

When I was in Leominster on business, I often stayed late and would take Joanne to dinner and many pleasant evenings were spent in the nearby Wheelbarrow Inn. This hostelry was a very oldie worldly pub, with an excellent menu and it gave us an opportunity to discuss the Proheat business and my plans for its future growth and I quickly saw my eldest developing and maturing into a much more self assured and confident young lady. The isolation from some of the unsavoury friends with whom she had been associating was one of my more astute moves.

When the Proheat lease was due to expire at Leominster, the search was on for new premises in Bristol, and after a quick round of the commercial property agents, I found new premises at Portway Road, Bristol, a good location, which was within sight of the M5 motorway. I appointed Mike King to manage this depot with Joanne as his assistant. By now, Joanne had a thorough knowledge of the whole product range and the lessons that she had learned about credit control with Mrs. Clegg were a valuable asset. She also grew in confidence as she accepted more responsibility, both within the branch and for her own life style.

While the stock and furniture was being moved from Leominster to Bristol I spent a weekend with Joanne flat hunting in Bristol, finally settling on a pleasant bed sit apartment almost overlooking the Downs, where she met some good friends who were sharing flats on the same floor as her. The flat was well located for easy access to the Portway Road depot. Several months later on my advice, she purchased a small two up two down semi detached house in Clevedon, just before the housing market value fell for the first time in several decades.

However, we enjoyed many happy times with family trips to the seaside visiting Joanne at weekends in her Clevedon home and many pleasant lunches were enjoyed in the Star Inn at Tickenham.

One other major change took place in Bristol a year later, as history was to repeat itself, when Mike King left Proheat after receiving his Christmas bonus and not returning in January, taking the driver Mike Turner with him to a competitor. It was not a great surprise that he left, as Mike always had a chip on his shoulder, which had caused an undercurrent of animosity with Mike that Joanne was the boss's daughter. But it did surprise me that any employee of management status would leave without giving notice and rule out any goodwill they may be required in seeking future employment. Mike did not last long with his new employer and Joanne went on to manage Proheat successfully for several years.

Her interest in Irish holidays was declining and her attraction for the city lights in Bristol was tarnishing her view of the Irish countryside. Michelle, on the other hand who was rather quiet and not at all adventurous, but her love for Ireland was so strong that at fourteen, caught a coach at Digbeth Coach Station and totally unaccompanied travelled by ferry and onward bus journey, changing in Waterford to Millstreet, where she was met by Aunt Kathleen. Something we would have been very reluctant to allow today.

Michelle had followed Joanne to Streetly Comprehensive School and was much more focused on her schoolwork and had a determination to succeed academically. She was eager to stay on to do 'A' levels and was soon to win the school science prize at the Prize Giving ceremony at Walsall Town Hall. Both Claire and

Kate also enjoyed their schooldays as pupils at Streetly High School as it had now been renamed.

Michelle left school with an ambition and determination to follow her mother's footsteps into nursing and was accepted as a student nurse to train at the Queen Elizabeth Hospital where she had been born. While waiting for the course to start, she accepted a job in a care home. Peter Pugh, a friend of mine, was associated with Orchard House Nursing Home situated in Whitehouse Common Road. This work would give her grounding in patient care, and Peter commented that if she could cope with working with geriatric patients in a Nursing Home, then she would find other areas of nursing a sinecure by comparison.

I was very pleased to see Michelle making her own way in life and away from the family business, especially as both Michelle and I had strong personalities and willpower, which may not have been the best recipe for an amicable working relationship at MMF.

At this time Rite Vent was becoming more conscious or more desperate than Selkirk to reduce MMF's extended credit and I received an invitation to the Rite Vent Factory in Washington to discuss the situation. Arrangements were made that John Hornby would collect me and take me to the Washington factory. Early that morning just before John arrived, I received a telephone call from my sister Connie, saying that she felt very ill with chest pains and could I come over. I explained that I was virtually on my way to Northumberland, but I assured her that Joan would call immediately after taking the children to school. By the time Joan arrived, the doctor had been and he had diagnosed acute indigestion. Joan stayed with her until she felt more comfortable and said the she would return after the school run. Joan returned to Connie after taking Joanne and Michelle to a gym class and Connie was no longer alive. It is difficult to believe now that any doctor could be so careless with such an incompetent diagnosis.

Joan was distraught and only had limited knowledge of my whereabouts. She knew that I had a meeting with Rite Vent in Washington and that I would be staying overnight, so she contacted Rite Vent and found that I was booked in to The Post House Hotel, Washington. She made an emergency call to the hotel and as I was sitting down to dinner, I was paged and Joan broke the shattering news of Connie's death. I was riddled with guilt that I had not responded to her plea for help that morning and a torrent of thoughts and options flooded through my mind.

John persuaded me that nothing could be achieved by rushing back that night and after a sleepless night mulling over a lifetime of memories and regrets, we journeyed south after an early breakfast the following day. I reflected on the journey that I had never been very close to Connie, as I was always more business like and had an engineering and practical disposition, whereas Connie had always been for the arts and culture. But Connie's loss came as a hard blow, as she was cremated at Perry Barr Crematorium following our Mother and Father. I was now the only survivor of my original family unit that had struggled through the war together unscathed.

Connie had spent most of her working life in a solicitor's office and it was not surprising that she had been meticulous in drawing up her will, which on reading the document I was disappointed to learn that my sister clearly wished to make a statement in drafting the document, as she had virtually excluded me and she must have harboured some feelings of which I was unaware, while she was alive. There was very little to bequeath, the estate was to be divided 50% to the solicitor that she worked for and the balance to be divided between her four nieces. The house at 143 Chipstead Road in which I had grown up, would have to be sold and the mortgage balance repaid and after the other debts cleared, the balance was very small and the girls inherited £250 each.

However, it did lead to a very pleasant weekend for Claire and I, as the house at Chipstead Road had to be cleared and whilst most of the furniture was quite old, some of it would be useful in the bungalow in Ireland. I used one of the company vans and booked the Swansea Ferry, Claire begged, could she come in the van with me, her appeals were so persistent that it was impossible to refuse. So with the van packed with the china cabinet that had originated from Cooksey Road and other furniture, carpets and a newly purchased sit on lawn mower we set off for the Emerald Isle. Claire carried a quiz book with her and had me attempting University Challenge all the way to Swansea. Claire always remembered that trip with much joy at having her me all to herself for a whole weekend and remarked later that that it was her most memorable trip to Ireland.

Quite a while after Connie's death, the meeting with Rite Vent was rescheduled and it became quite clear to me that this could well turn into an ambush situation. MMF was still very indebted to them, in part due to the consignment stock, but also by their own incompetence.

John Hornby in his capacity as Rite Vents sales executive would provide special terms to secure the flue business on particular contracts, mainly with flexible flue liner, which he would notify his office on a specially prepared form. Whether by incompetence or accident, when the goods were invoiced the special terms were rarely included. I always dealt with the Rite Vent and Selkirk payments myself, because of the complications that these deals brought with them and I would withhold payment of any invoices that were incorrect until the invoice could be matched with the appropriate credit note.

Due to my suspicions that the meeting was more about the credit situation than a social visit, I spent several days preparing for the meeting and listed all of the invoices that were incorrect and required credit notes, with notations by the side of each entry as to why it had not been paid. On arrival in Washington, I had been booked into The Post House Hotel again, which rekindled the sad memories of the earlier visit. I was wined and dined very hospitably, but the meeting that followed the next morning, was, as I had expected, a totally different proposition.

Assembled before me was a posse of big guns, including their senior accountant, Paul Gordon a director, John Bradley the sales director and John Hornby. In fairness, John had pre-warned them to have their case well prepared because he was well aware of my ability in these situations and he, the consummate salesman that he was, said very little during the meeting and was happy to observe the proceedings and even left the meeting at one stage in embarrassment. The meeting became very heated with me outlining all of the difficulties and my time being consumed in checking Rite Vent invoices, because of the high percentage of errors that I would rather that they would take all of their stock back and I would happily trade without them.

This was a huge bluff, but it brought John Bradley to his feet with forceful vehemence, saying that they would not accept any stock back and this was all a ploy by me to avoid or delay payment, there was no way so many invoices could be wrong. I let him have his little tirade, before reaching into my brief case and producing my well prepared list and fired off mistake after mistake in their invoicing procedures and hinted that, maybe they were not mistakes at all. Eventually when the extent of their incompetence had been ground home item by item, they apologised to me and a few months later the accountant was either sacked or left. John Hornby drove himself and me back to Birmingham and although little was said about the meeting, as John's loyalties had to be to his employer, I could not help feeling like the Lone Grainger in a cowboy film who had shot down the entire posse.

It was also about this time that my interest in music was rekindled, when one Saturday morning Joan wanted me to travel into the city to buy a new gas cooker. I was never much of a shopper and became distracted when looking through a shop window at electric organs. My mind raced back to my accordion days and believed with my knowledge of chords and ability to read music, one of these instruments could be quickly mastered. Three days later, a Yamaha organ was delivered and after some lessons and several organs later, I became quite proficient. This led to a mega project when I paid a substantial amount for a self build Wersi kit and spent months soldering circuit boards to complete this state of the art instrument. However, like all technology within a few years' better instruments, at much less cost, superseded it. Incidentally it was several months before a new cooker arrived.

CHAPTER FOURTEEN

Hillsborough

Selkirk was always a prolific entertainer their representatives having substantial budgets to provide hospitality to their customers and one of the highlights of the football season was the reservation of two seats in the Selkirk hospitality box at Nottingham Forest Stadium for the Liverpool game. I was still an ardent Birmingham City supporter, but Michelle, my fourteen year old daughter, was even more fanatical about Liverpool and in particular Kenny Dalglish, her bedroom walls were almost wall to wall posters of the team and her Liverpool heroes.

I had taken Michelle to Anfield earlier in the year and had stood on the Kop for the very first time to experience an atmosphere, which is a unique phenomenon with scousers at Anfield. The vast crowd overawed Michelle due to her small stature and the pushing, in the then seat less stand, made it difficult for her to enjoy the game. But the box at the City Ground with Cloughy at his peak and Forest versus the Pool was a gargantuan game to watch in the comfort of the hospitality suite. The teams were also destined to meet again a few weeks later in the F.A. Cup semi final at Hillsborough and I asked Alan Kirby the area sales manager, could he get tickets for the semi final and Alan confirmed later that week, that he had two tickets for me.

Saturday morning 15th April 1989 and the F.A. Cup semi final day arrived. Michelle and I set off for Sheffield, parking just over a mile away from the Hillsborough Stadium and at least an hour and a half before kick off. We strolled down towards the stadium with many excited supporters and then took our seats just to the right of centre of the main stand, with the Leppings Road Stand on our left, to await the kick off while munching chocolates and reading the programme from cover to cover. The clock slowly ticked round to three o'clock, with excitement building to fever pitch, the teams kicked off and the semi final underway, but it was a match that was to last only six minutes, before the players were taken back off the field.

We were both mystified; was there crowd trouble, had Cloughie blown a fuse, was the referee sick? The minutes ticked away and gradually the police formed a human barrier across the centre line. Supporters were tearing down advertising hoardings, it was rumoured for stretchers, but still no announcement as to what was happening or why the game had not restarted. We were unable to see any of the carnage that was happening at the rear of the Leppings Road stand, other than a few people being helped up from below into the upper stand. Eventually, at least an hour after kick off, Kenny Dalglish's Scottish dialect boomed out over the tannoy speakers, the game had been abandoned, due to serious injuries and fatalities within the ground. He asked everyone to stay in their seats to ensure that the emergency service vehicles would not be hampered in getting casualties to hospital. This had been quite a brief statement that had brought such an eagerly awaited day to a stunning and disappointing conclusion.

We stayed in the ground as instructed until five o'clock and it was only as we left the ground and saw a sea of ambulances around the exit that the magnitude of the disaster was beginning to dawn upon us. Joan and the rest of the family at home were frantic, they had seen the graphic television pictures that neither Michelle nor I could see. They were much more aware of the devastation and carnage that had been happening for the last hour. They were thinking 'Why had Tom not made contact, they must be injured or worse?' We strolled back to the car and using the car phone, finally called home to be bombarded with tears and questions and finally relief. It was not until we saw the extensive television coverage of the disaster on returning home in the evening that we realised that we had witnessed what must be the greatest ever football tragedy, which even eclipsed the disaster that had occurred four years earlier at the Heysel Stadium, that had cost the lives of 35 supporters.

We were able to exchange Hillsborough tickets for the replay, which was to be played at Old Trafford and we both made our first visit to the home of Manchester United to see the game, which Liverpool won. The Pool also then went on to beat Everton at Wembley 3-2 after extra time, but this was little consolation for the families of the 96 fans killed at Hillsborough and the whole family reflected on what might have happened if our tickets had located us differently, at the Hillsborough Stadium.

Nineteen Eighty Nine also brought celebrations for Rite Vent and to commemorate their twenty first birthday, they booked a grand banquet in the 11th Century Durham Castle and invited many of their top customers to celebrate with them, including me. Our earlier differences had long since been repaired because despite the earlier spat and threats, both companies needed each other in equal proportions.

The Castle had been given to the Durham University in the 1840s, but the mediaeval backdrop in the banqueting hall created a spectacular setting for the evening's celebrations. The meal was followed by congratulatory speeches and the main guest speaker was Barry Took, a BBC celebrity. The whole event was a pleasant opportunity to meet many old friends and competitors. The milestone celebrations were enhanced with a round of golf the following day and I must say that the scoring was not great, due to everyone's concentration being a little blurred with more than a few hangovers.

The end of the eighties brought a change in the economy, banks were becoming much more cautious with lending and although the MMF Group of companies was still growing healthily, both in turnover and profit, it would not stop the bank's blinkered approach to reducing their exposure to lending. This caused a major problem for me, when the bank announced that they wanted to reduce my company's overdraft facility from £750,000 to £550,000 effectively taking £200,000 out of the cash flow. I questioned why they would want to move the goalposts so drastically, the cover for their debt was greater now than when the facility had been granted, but this was a time when the old experienced bank managers had become dinosaurs and been replaced by graduate whiz kids. This new generation of bankers were mathematicians, with little understanding of commerce and with only a modicum of business acumen, but had the authority to weald an axe indiscriminately.

I hastily arranged meetings with Selkirk's financial director and with John Garrard, Rite Vent's CEO, who was the founder of the company I explained the stance that the bank was taking and that it had no reasoned substance and asked for their support. I needed the 30 days credit terms to be extended to 60 days, if I was to continue without a massive step backward. They both valued MMF as a customer who was spending huge sums of money with them each month. Whilst they were not overwhelmed by the idea, it was preferred to losing a vast amount of business. However, a large Selkirk debt became even larger, to the extent that they were acting as second banker, quite a dangerous position for my company to become ensconced, but the bank had made it Hobson's choice.

Other cutbacks were essential, the biggest casualty causing me most regret was Alan Kirby, who at my instigation had left a secure pensioned career with Selkirk to join MMF, but the salvation of other jobs had to take priority and Alan's departure would bring a substantial saving with his combined salary, expenses and company car and was a sacrifice that had to be made. Mrs. Clegg together with her company car had to go, but she was looking forward to retirement in any case and was quite pleased that the decision had been taken for her. Another casualty was John Maccata, who was on a £12,000 a year retainer plus expenses, so he was also axed, but with little regret, as he had not been able to achieve the objective that he had been employed for.

These combined redundancies created a total saving approaching £100,000 a year in overheads and were necessary to impress the misguided bankers and ensure that they did not get any more penal in their approach to the financial arrangements with MMF.

Whilst this was a huge set back and was to change my growth plans for nearly a decade, it did have some advantages. The increased overdraft for the Proheat acquisition had cost MMF almost a hundred thousand pounds in interest in a single year, in fact the entire profits for that year. We had in effect worked all year for the bank. The reduction in overdraft facility was replaced by free credit from our suppliers. This, together with the saving in overheads, swiftly increased our post tax profitability, which would set the correct course to stabilise the cash flow quite quickly.

A bad run of fortune deteriorated further, when a VAT inspection discovered a flaw in the way cash sales were being processed, as some of the cash from cash sales was being used for petty cash purchases, but the company had failed to record these transactions in accordance with the VAT requirements. When all of the petty cash receipts could not be produced, it resulted in a heavy estimated claw back by the Customs and Excise and penalties and interest were added. In addition, the Inland Revenue wanted their pound of flesh and the resultant cost to the company was a further loss to the cash flow, to the order of sixty thousand pounds. I asked Terry if he would join me in raising a mortgage on our homes, to redress the hole that this Revenue demand had made in the cash flow. Terry's salary was increased to cover the increase in his mortgage repayments and I awarded him some shares in the company, in acknowledgement of his loyalty in helping me out of this embarrassing situation.

This unpleasant episode at last convinced me that I needed to employ an accountant, something I had never done before, as I never held them in very high regard and had always produced my own accounts, with the help of a powerful computer accounting package.

This brought Tony Beard to MMF, as he wished to leave his current employer, Starbuck Stone and Co., the company's auditors, soon after he had completed the routine forensic work for the audit. Although he was not chartered, by doing all of the preparation work for the annual audit he had gained a sound knowledge of the company's accounts, and I was happy to bring him on board.

Joanne was now managing the Bristol office and had already added new friends in Bristol while enjoying a very good social life and one of the parties had brought her into contact with a certain Ken Rogers. It was not too long before Joanne had been swept off her feet by this Bristolian and with her usual sense of timing, announced her engagement, to the now infamous Ken Rogers. Her fiancé' had been employed by his parents working in the rest home as a care assistant/cook that they owned and managed. This raised some concerns with me and I was prompted to talk to her about her future with him, as to what standard of living and home comforts she was expecting from her husband to be, but she was in love and love would conquer all.

The wedding was booked at St. Bonaventure's Catholic Church in Bristol for 7th October 1990, just seven days before our own twenty fifth wedding anniversary was due and at a time when I could least afford an ostentatious wedding for my eldest and first daughter to be wed. Ken had insisted on a Top Hat and Tails wedding, with a modest pub reception, which was followed by a huge disco at the County Ground home of the Gloucestershire County Cricket Club. Joanne had asked Michelle, Claire and Kate to be her bridesmaids and a combined effort by Joan, myself and the Rogers family provided a buffet for the evening celebrations.

The wedding was a disaster for many reasons, logistically it was difficult being in Bristol, but it deteriorated further, when Joan discovered that I had only packed half of her wedding outfit, which had been bought with all of the thought and care that any mother would want for her first daughters wedding, at a stage that was irrecoverable, even using a despatch rider. She must have loved me very much that I survived to tell the tale, even joking about it in my speech. After the honeymoon Joanne and Ken settled down to live in her house in Clevedon.

I made another useful contact that would make a significant contribution to our profitability, again it was the MEB, but this time it was Clive Houston who would had moved quickly up the ranks, with the departure of Clive Taylor, when he left to start Exeway. The MEB was about to build a new enlarged two winged office block, each wing having three storeys. This new head office, was to be fully air conditioned and Clive asked me to do the drawings and carry out all of the duct sizing on the project, based on the refrigeration loads calculated by Clive, and in return MMF would be awarded the contract to manufacture and install all of the ductwork, it was inferred that there would be no competition for the project. I estimated that the cost would be in excess of £40,000 with the MEB providing all of the air conditioning plant. This was accepted and I was more than pleased with the profit margin.

Selkirk was also ringing the changes with the departure of Ron Buttery, which was a huge disappointment to me, but his successor David Jones was a friend from the past, as David had been Southern area sales manager, at the time when Proheat was moved from Leominster to Bristol. We quickly re-established a good relationship and this appointment created an opportunity for Alan Kirby to return to Selkirk, when Dana Davis left rather unceremoniously.

Tony Beard's arrival at MMF as our accountant was to signal the departure of Joan, who had always helped out when I was under pressure, mainly with accounts work, or any other clerical work that needed her attention, but she could not get on with Tony and told me after only a short time that she could not work with that man, which was very strong language for Joan. At the same time Claire had found a Saturday job at St. Martin's care home, as a care assistant, which turned into full time work, while she was waiting to start her Nursing Diploma.

When the proprietors were about to open a Nursing Home in Vesey Road and were looking for qualified staff Claire tried to convince Joan to apply for one of the many nursing posts that were on offer, she knew that Joan wanted to get back to her first love of nursing, but lacked confidence, claiming that everything had moved on since she had last nursed a patient. But Claire brimming with confidence and pride in her mother, arranged an interview and Joan returned to nursing, first as a sister and later appointed deputy matron, a post that she held for several years.

She left St. Martins after the current Matron left. It came about when she applied for the vacant matron post, but a new matron was appointed from one of her subordinates. Joan had always put the priority of the patients before Nursing Home profits and was now in an untenable position and resigned to avoid any conflict of interest. She was quickly snapped up by BUPA at Aston Court Nursing Home in Little Aston and happily accepted a sisters post and enjoyed working in a larger, more professional organisation nearer to home.

MMF's era at Clement Street was coming to an end, when the landlord Cookson, the publicly quoted metals company, sold the property to Wimpey Construction, who lost no time in notifying us that they wanted to re-develop the total site, which included the MMF premises. I contacted the company solicitors, but I was advised that it could not be opposed but Wimpey would have to pay MMF compensation.

The compensation would more than cover the cost of the move and would be a welcome addition to the cash flow. I quickly found new premises at Alma Street, off Soho Way, which were not as aesthetically inspiring or convenient as Clement Street, as they were split on two sides of the road. On the right hand side was the factory building with car parking space and on the other side of the road, a very tall Victorian three-storey building, 'Alma Works' which with mezzanine floors added, gave ample storage area, but both premises had limited office space.

I purchased the factory premises myself and leased

them back to the company and the pension fund bought the Victorian building and also entered into a lease agreement. Ron Foster and the contracting company were more suited to the offices over the factory and the sales office and admin staff, together with Tony Beard and I were all accommodated on the first floor of the Alma Works building. We moved lock, stock and barrel over two weekends, with all hands to the pump, including both Terry and me humping and driving the van with the rest the of lads and to much banter and camaraderie, finishing in the pub, with me buying drinks all round in appreciation for a great team effort.

All of the head office staff was now safely ensconced in the Alma Street premises and Tony Beard was working hard introducing extra control systems and staggering in and out of the office each day with a bread tray full of box files. He totally reorganised the filing system so that all old records could be easily located.

CHAPTER FIFTEEN

More Additions

I received a call from Mrs. Flowers our landlord at the Mansfield property advising me that she was going to sell the Victoria Street premises, but as sitting tenants she wanted to give us first refusal. She invited me to her house, to a very nicely prepared home made lunch, before allowing any talk about the property. But after lunch was finished, this elderly self assured lady explained with great authority, that there would be no negotiation, the price she wanted was £55,000 which was more than reasonable as I had expected to pay much more. I accepted her offer and arranged a mortgage with Lloyds Bank and the Mansfield premises became a Fixed Asset on the company books. Only a few years later it was re valued at £125,000.

Soon after the purchase of the Mansfield premises, I became interested in a company based in Oldbury, who carried out work for Selkirk on free standing chimneys and multiple steel chimneys that required supporting masts. The company, Wrights Technical Services Ltd., (WTS) which, really only comprised of Mervin Wright, his draughtsman Peter Rose and an office Girl Friday, Irene, although Irene would have been very flattered by this description, as she was a very mature lady. But Mervin was a chartered structural engineer and not only provided some of the structural calculations for Selkirk, but had a history dating back to Dunkirk with temporary structures for the evacuation.

Although I had put further major expansion plans on hold to concentrate on our organic growth with the objective of reducing our dependence on what I saw as a capricious and indiscriminate banking system, I found WTS an irresistible attraction. By combining the excellent contracts department that Ron Foster had built up with the vast experience and abounding technical skills that Mervin Wright could bring, a very comprehensive design and installation service could be provided. I offered Mervin £70,000 to acquire his company and expertise, providing that he would stay on for at least two years. WTS was a profitable company and by moving the personnel from Oldbury to the Alma street offices, savings would be made on the overheads. We completed the acquisition with letters of exchange between solicitors and few professional costs.

The combination of Ron Foster and Mervin Wright was an instant success, as they both gelled from the first day, both having a great respect for each other; Mervin for Ron's energy and dedication to his work and Ron for Mervin's ability and knowledge of structures. Mervin would carry out most of the design work and calculations, while Ron who was learning a great deal from him, would do most of the project management.

Many substantial orders were won by this team including a 30 metre high by 1.5 metre diameter, freestanding steel chimney with aircraft warning lights and lightening conductor at RAF Brize Norton and triple stainless steel chimneys supported by a lattice mast at the NEC. In addition, many local projects that can still be seen today at the Dental Hospital and Severn Trent offices, as well as the multi boilers house conversions and updates of the old General Hospital to the Children's Hospital.

The MMF Group at this stage in their development was a collection of separate companies, which necessitated separate accounts, separate audits and separate payrolls. All companies were producing good profits and our indebtedness to the bank was reducing annually and when the corporation tax juggling with counter charges between companies was becoming tiresome and more difficult to justify, a case was made to re structure this fragmented group of companies.

Mike Rudd and Co., now our companies' auditors, recommended that all of the companies should be hived up into one company and Tony Beard together with the other directors all agreed to what turned out to be a lengthy and complicated process. The hive up began with most of the work falling on Tony Beard's shoulders, providing information for the solicitors and negotiations with the Inland Revenue and after several months, MMF Midlands Ltd., MMF Northern Ltd., MMF Manufacturing Ltd., Proheat Ltd. and Wrights Technical Services Ltd., all simply became MMF Ltd.

A further addition to our product range came with a visit of Lars Hanson, a representative from a Danish company, Exhausto. They had been manufacturing chimney fans for several years and had been exporting them to many European countries. Their representative was approaching all of the specialist flue distributors in

Britain to set up a distribution network for their products. I saw this as a welcome addition to our range of products and readily agreed to a mutual working arrangement that would see the introduction and sales of their products throughout all of our depots.

Exhausto arranged to fly me, together with a number of other prospective distributors, from their various locations from Birmingham to Billund and then by coach to their Langeskof factory just east of Odense. The visit was to last two days, the first seeing the products being made with a tour of their extensive modern factory and the second allocated to training, in the sizing of the fans for different applications.

We were all warmly welcomed and had been booked into a very comfortable hotel. Next we were to be treated to a typical Danish banquet of forty shades of herring. I had never seen so many herring dishes in my life. While growing up my father had drooled over the delicacy of soused herring, but the array before me was without question mind blowing; curried herrings, herrings in jam, herrings in wine, in fact herrings in almost anything imaginable washed down with Aquavit, the Danish equivalent of the German Schnapps. I have to admit that this was not one of my finest hours as far as cuisine was concerned, but the generosity behind the hospitality was gratefully received.

The training for the fan sizing came fairly easy to me, with my technical background and my command of maths, but the instructor was inspired to make an amusing comment while I was carrying out conversions from metric to imperial units, for the calculations when he said, 'The biggest trouble with you English, you will only go metric inch by inch.' Before leaving the factory

I placed a stock order and the party returned home suitably impressed. The stock range was not great and the Exhausto products produced a steady stream of high margin sales.

On the home front Michelle had completed her Nursing Diploma and had moved to Ireland, working for a Japanese electronics company Alps, as she was unable to secure a nursing post in Ireland without a qualification in the Irish Language, but there was a much bigger attraction in Ireland, a certain Michael Smyth. Claire had also completed her Nursing Diploma and after six months in the eye department at Sandwell Hospital, had applied for and secured a post at the Cottage Hospital in Sutton Coldfield, caring for stroke patients and helping to rehabilitate them. She loved the job, travelling around assessing patient's needs and running a falls clinic, teaching stroke patients how to get themselves up if they fell and how to care for themselves in their own homes, but she had started to experience some niggling health problems and hospital visits were becoming more regular.

By September 1992 when the UK crashed out of the ERM so ignominiously, the American owners of Selkirk were putting them under much greater pressure to reduce their receivables, in the UK terms these would have been creditors, of which MMF was one of several companies that were heavily indebted to them. I was summoned to a meeting at the Holiday Inn Hotel in Bristol to a sandwich and coffee lunch, worlds apart from the lavish lunches that were usually showered on customers of MMF standing.

Dick Horsfall, their general manager, who I had met socially on many occasions and Brian Greenslade their financial controller were the inquisitors. The atmosphere, while friendly was intense, as they wished to stress the seriousness of the situation and to emphasise that something had to be done to reduce the debt. I started by saying that I could fully understand their position, but explained that it was their own successive sales directors that had created the current situation and that it was not something that I could resolve quickly, without doing serious damage to the sales of both of our companies.

They were not really convinced and I had to explain that I had no magic wand or treasure chest to dip into. If they wanted a quick fix, then I only had three alternatives I could reduce my purchases from Selkirk and sell off existing stocks, but this would have a detrimental effect on my own and thereby Selkirk customers; I could take the same line as Selkirk with our own customers and reduce their credit, which would also result in a reduction in sales for both companies and the third option and the least palatable to Selkirk, was for them to offer bigger discounts to MMF and thereby increase our profit margins and thus reduce the debt to Selkirk more quickly out of profits.

None of these alternatives was acceptable but it was agreed that both companies would let things stand for the time being, the situation would be kept under close scrutiny and I agreed to make every effort to reduce the debt year on year out of the profits, as they were being generated. I drove back up the M5 motorway heaving a huge sigh of relief as yet another potential banana skin had been avoided.

However, The Specialist Flue Company in Suffolk managed by Neil Fry was taking a much more aggressive approach to an identical situation. He resented that Selkirk was controlling, to a large extent, the products that he could sell. He had his own manufacturing facility similar to me, but started selling his own products aggressively, in direct opposition to his major supplier, to whom he was heavily indebted. I was surprised at the line that Neil was taking, but he was a man of great experience in the flue industry and obviously had an agenda of his own.

I was not surprised that Selkirk took exception to Neil's stance finding themselves helping to finance what had the potential to become a substantial competitor to them in the South East area of the country. It was not long before Selkirk took some action and to the amazement of the whole trade, sent a number of forty-foot containers to Suffolk, to recoup stock and reduce the extent of the debt and stopped all further supplies. This effectively put The Specialist Flue Company out of business and at great loss to both companies.

Possibly Neil Fry, who had a wealth of experience in the flue industry and a deep technical knowledge, had gambled that this would not happen, bearing in mind that The Specialist Flue Company was buying in excess of 1.2 million pounds worth of product from Selkirk each year, at that time, or possibly he decided that Selkirk could go to hell and he would do his own thing with a new company, though I still wonder why it was not possible to negotiate a settlement that would have been much more beneficial to both companies.

It was a huge customer for Selkirk to lose and possibly an unrecoverable debt, but it did send a signal out to the other Selkirk creditors to keep in line. Whilst I got the message, I did not believe that Selkirk could afford to repeat this operation with another big customer. In retrospect my sigh of relief at my diplomatic skills when I drove up the motorway after my meeting with Horsfield and Greenslade was well founded.

However, life goes on and Neil Fry the founder of The Specialist Flue Company together with his son Darren continued business with commercial flue installations, with a new company The Specialist Flue Service Ltd. Jeremy Fry, Neil's other son, who was, and still is, very well respected in the flue business, picked up the pieces of the now extinct company and started Specflue Ltd. and MMF followed Rite Vent, who had stayed loyal to Jeremy, in supplying his new company when Selkirk refused to deal with them.

Both MMF and Specflue generated a substantial amount of business over the next few years in Suffolk and the surrounding areas and when I needed to upgrade our computer system, which was now twelve years old, I turned to Jeremy, who had installed a Castle System, which was much more sophisticated than our equipment and software and as a result IBM hardware and the Castle software were installed at Birmingham, Mansfield, and Bristol, all interlinked by modem connections.

All of the computers could communicate with each other, stock checks and availability was instantly accessible at all branches, integrated stock movement and automatic reordering was possible, which together with more detailed sales and stock valuation reports gave us much greater control over the company's management systems when coupled to the accounting package. We leased all of the system over five years and the effect on cash flow was minimal.

Tony Beard was delighted with the new computer equipment and worked tirelessly to adapt the software and tailor it to MMF's needs. Within a few months, he was able to produce quite detailed monthly management accounts for each division of the company.

He also created a series of integrated, self calculating spreadsheets, for various elements of the accounts, the wages in particular was very creative, in that by extracting information from the reports that the computer spewed out, he could cross check the PAYE and NI for each division and also have an accurate calculation for the Revenue payments. He also compiled an asset register on the spreadsheet in addition to calculations comparing actual sales against budgets for the board meetings. Having had an audit background, he was able to present the accounts and audit trails in the form that the auditors would require, all documented on detailed spreadsheets.

At Selkirk, major changes were also taking place, probably caused by their parent company, Elger Industries in America, who had been forced into Chapter Eleven, similar to administration in the UK. Even though the company was basically sound, a law suit involving a faulty product could have had multi million dollar consequences had it gone against them.

The whole situation was very complicated, as there were counter claims against Household Manufacturing a previous owner. One of the results of this litigation was eventually to coincide with the downfall of John Botton, the UK Chief Executive of Selkirk. John had always been a bit of a recluse, but in spite of this, he was a very polished individual with a commanding disposition and had a very focused marketing strategy. He was already a legend in the flue industry and his departure was to signal the beginning of the end for Selkirk in the UK.

It was hinted that the Elger Industries problems in America were overstated and Elger shares might be a good gamble at $8 per share. The shares were still being traded, even while under Chapter Eleven, I took a big gamble and opened a dollar trading account with Lloyds and bought into Elger. I happened to mention this to a long standing friend, Geoff Bannister, who also said he wouldn't mind a punt himself. Geoff then told John Husband a golfing friend and before long, some wild gambling was taking place, much to my consternation.

Suffice to say, it all turned out OK and we all lived happy ever after, when Elger was eventually sold for $25 per share, most of my friends had bought shares at between $8 and $9.

John Botton's successor at Selkirk was Mike Moran, a broad and somewhat brash Yorkshire man, with an engineering background in engines, exactly what that meant no one was quite sure, but he certainly did not understand the somewhat incestuous nature of flue business and made it clear that he did not want to. He was going to revolutionise the way Selkirk did business. What he had failed to recognise was that John Botton had taken a very ordinary basic stainless steel sheet metal product and by superb and industrious marketing, had convinced the heating industry that his products were the elite of all flue systems available. In addition to this, his relationship with John Garrard his competitor was such that between them, they had kept the prices of their respective products high and very profitable.

Mike Moran, with his blind bulldog approach, virtually declared war on Rite Vent, sending out the message to his sales force that he wanted to take as much of their market share as possible, and whilst this had always been the case, Selkirk had been much more subtle in their approach under Botton. Moran was now preparing to make flexible flue liner, which had been one of the preserves that Botton had left to his competitor, as it was low cost and a very competitive product.

The new approach and initiatives provided me with a great opportunity, to not only regain some business that was being taken by John Hornby, who was now selling some Rite Vent products direct to some of my existing merchant customers, but also to buy Selkirk products at better discounts and thereby increase our profitability, something that had not been possible when I met with Horsfall and Greenslade in Bristol.

This came about when Dave Jones appointed Kevin Samuels as national sales manager. Kevin was a very jovial and likeable character with a grinning moustache that helped to light up his face, but he was new to the flue business and came across as being a little naïve. This appointment was not popular with all of Selkirk's distributors, in fact Docherty's in Reading were quite hostile towards him. I recognised that Kevin had great power under the new regime and that the bread of life for salesmen was sales, not necessarily profitability, quite the opposite to my own doctrine.

The new directive to take Rite Vent business almost at any cost to Selkirk, gave me the chance, by cultivating my relationship with Kevin and together with Alan Kirby the local representative, negotiated special discounts to target Rite Vent customers that were not trading with MMF, for conversion to Selkirk. However Selkirk had no way of knowing how much or exactly where these special discounts were being applied and the temptation to inflate these 'special purchases' was too great an opportunity to resist, especially when considering Moran's extrovert attitude to marketing.

This led to an unpleasant confrontation at the Selkirk factory, when I met Barry Morecroft the MD of Docherty's, when Barry accused me of bribing Kevin, and stating loudly that Kevin was in my pocket. How could MMF sell at the discounts that were being offered?

These statements were totally untrue and slanderous. What Barry had not realised was that while he was constantly belittling Kevin and telling everyone how inadequate he was I was cultivating a stronger relationship with him with monthly lunch time meetings at Selkirk's expense, usually in Henry Wong's in St Paul's Square and leading him to deals that were doable. I would have called this business acumen and was only too happy to have Barry huffing and puffing, while the gift horse was staring at his blindfold.

The introduction of Selkirk into the flexible flue market was obviously a cause of concern to their Rite Vent competitor, especially as MMF was currently buying all their flex from them. I discovered by accident that Rite Vent were selling flexible flue products to the gas board at a better price than I could buy, for much lower volumes of business.

This caused me to change my buying policy immediately and with the aid of the Castle computer I was able to print out our annual purchases of flue liner and I proceeded to invite tenders for an annual supply contract. The invitations were sent to Rite Vent, Turner and Wilson and Selkirk, the three big players in this market.

This supply contract would represent a vast amount of business for a single product line, certainly in excess of £350,000 per annum. Turner and Wilson was the successful bidder and their improved price would considerably increase our profitability and ability to compete for a bigger market share in the coming year. Before an order was placed, John Hornby, who had no intention of losing the business, asked if he could negotiate on Rite Vent's behalf and I agreed. John reported back to his sales director and told them that if they did not negotiate better terms, they would lose this business. They obviously thought that my poker hand was a bluff and said that they could see no reason to improve their bid.

Two months later, when they had not received any orders for flexible flue liner from MMF, the proverbial excrement hit the fan and John was summoned to Washington to explain why his sales figures had dropped so dramatically. John in no uncertain words told them that he had given them the chance to retain the MMF flex business and his bosses had ignored the consequences. Why were they now so surprised at the drop in sales? They asked him what they had to do to recover the business.

His curt response was 'Don't ask me, ask Tom.'

A phone call from Roy Stabler, John's boss quickly followed, they would match the Turner and Wilson price and increase MMF's annual rebate to a maximum 7% retrospectively, this would mean that not only would I be buying my flex at less cost, but also all of the other Rite Vent products. I unfairly used the excuse of a late delivery from our new supplier to return the business to Rite Vent. At this time Selkirk's flex production was still in its infancy and they were having difficulty in overcoming production problems so they were not really an option in any case.

The combined effect of the Selkirk and Rite Vent hostility to each other was music to my ears, our profits increased to the extent, that in a single year I had to put a very substantial amount into the pension fund to reduce the corporation tax liability money that was partly re-loaned back to the company to maintain the cash flow. It was also at this time that I gave a few shares to Tony Beard in recognition of his efforts, hoping to instil a degree of loyalty to a pivotal member of staff. The debt with Selkirk was reducing to the extent that settlement discounts were being added to the annual profit pot.

MMF was now generating double digit growth annually, both in turnover and profitability and all elements of the business were gathering momentum. My only real concern was with WTS, as I was reluctant to let the contracting element of the business get too big as a ratio to the total group turnover. I knew from my early days all of the potential problems with contracting, retentions being held, often for years, on site disputes, and control of on site labour, were all ways that money could be lost. I directed them to concentrate their efforts on profitability rather than growth, with these factors in mind.

Exciting and welcome news arrived from Bristol, when Joanne announced that we could look forward to our first grandchild. The pregnancy went well, despite our concerns about Joanne's diabetic condition and on the 22nd May 1993 a son Jack arrived. This really was something special for me, a grandson as I was of the opinion that only little girls were available after my own experiences. Jack was a little jaundiced at birth, but after a short stay in the Special Care Baby Unit at Southmead Hospital, he was allowed home and was the pride and joy of his Grandparents. We spent the weekend in Clevedon travelling daily to support Joanne and to stare in wonderment at the new arrival.

We had to recruit a new manager in Bristol. Neil Jewell was the successful applicant and a year later Joanne put the Clevedon house up for sale with the intention of returning to Birmingham with husband Ken and son Jack. The housing market had sill not recovered and the house was slow to sell. There was no shortage of space in Middleton Road, as Michelle had already qualified as a nurse and had moved to Ireland to be near Michael, her husband to be.

The little Rogers family stayed with us in Streetly, before finding a house that they could afford and made an offer for a house in George Road, Erdington almost facing Brookvale Park It required some redecoration work, but possibly Ken would soon have it restored to its full glory. I had found a job for Ken in the factory and Joanne took control of the sales ledger and credit control for the group, working from home with a computer link to all branches. The time that Ken spent with us had started to ring warning bells in our ears.

It became very obvious that he was very fond of the booze, he was very immature and had a problem telling the truth, but for all his faults Jo and Jack were mad about him, as he had a happy go lucky carefree personality. Sadly, only a short time later, after they had decided to move house and together with the birth of their second child Katie, on the 21st May 1995, all the responsibility became a bit too much for him and he walked out and he found refuge with his mother back in Bristol, never to return. The departure had a devastating effect on Jack who was only four and left him feeling very insecure, but Katie who was only a few months old never really missed him at all.

Jo was devastated at the time, but was later relieved when she found the depths that he had sunk to. In addition it would later open the door to a new relationship with Richard. The timing could not have been worse, as they were in the process of moving house at the time. The sale of the George Road property had been agreed and an offer for a beautiful house in Minstead Road had been accepted. I convinced Joanne to press ahead with the move, as this would help if a divorce came to fruition.

Our thirtieth wedding anniversary was approaching and I wanted to arrange something special, as Joanne's wedding had overshadowed our twenty-fifth anniversary celebrations. I booked a short holiday in Rome to be followed by a longer spell in Sorrento. The few days in Rome would coincide with the actual date of our marriage thirty years previous and we would celebrate Mass in St Peter's at 11am, followed by a tour of the Sistine Chapel and after a candle lit dinner, a trip to see the Trevi fountains by floodlight. The following day we toured the Coliseum, before travelling to a fabulous hotel in Sorrento, where we basked in the Italian sunshine by the pool, when not touring the Isle of Capri and the Amalfi Coast.

CHAPTER SIXTEEN

MMF moves to Smethwick

The growth of the company in all directions was causing many logistical problems both in the factory and warehouse space and I decided to look for larger and more suitable premises. I started by making contact with a number of commercial property agents advising them of a specification of our requirements. We required at least 30,000 sq.ft, all had to be on the ground floor, with the exception of the offices and with good road side access and parking.

Cook Rudling forwarded, amongst many properties details of factory and warehouse premises in Woodburn Road, Smethwick, which had a floor area of 45,000 sq ft., with a very large frontage and excellent access, together with ample first floor office space. The asking price had been reduced over several years from £400,000 to £275,000. It was in a very poor state of repair and was costing the current owner great expense in security and insurance. Tony Beard made the point that this was a regeneration area and grants may well be available to modernise the building. I made an offer of £175,000 and without any haggle, it was accepted. We then raised a mortgage with Lloyds Bank, by now cover in the way of assets was not an issue and the purchase went ahead.

Tony pursued the possibility of a regeneration grant and after much negotiation with Sandwell Council a grant of £30,000 was offered, but this was only part of the £125,000 that it would cost to replace the roof, reinstate the factory floor, which was badly damaged after heavy machinery had been removed by the previous owner IMI, plus the replacement of all of the first floor office windows and redecoration. We had to appoint an architect under the terms of the grant and quotations were invited for the refurbishment work.

There was no great urgency to leave the Alma Street premises, as both our pension fund and myself were the current landlords, although MMF's departure would leave me with two empty buildings to sell or lease. I put both buildings on the market with Cook Rudling awaiting a buyer, while the rents continued to swell the pension fund.

In the period between buying the Woodburn Road property and the building being ready for occupation, a number of significant things were happening. I started to look at a company in the Suffolk area called B-Line, it was managed by an ex-employee of the old Specialist Flue Company, Chris Bartlett and although it was purely engaged in commercial flue installation, I saw it as a possible base for a new depot that came with a competent manager. I made an outline offer but I did not pursue it, mainly because so much else was going on with the move.

My relationship with Tony Beard was becoming strained, the prospect of another branch would increase his workload and he was insisting that he needed a personal assistant. He had junior staff checking purchase invoices and other general routine clerical duties, but he was getting carried away with too much detail. He was able to produce figures for every vehicle, what it had cost in fuel and maintenance and all sorts of other minor details which were time consuming and costing more to produce and record the information than I believed that it was worth. There was also friction between Terry and Tony in how the Birmingham branch was being managed. My mind went back to the early days of the management consultant and accountants building their own empires. The cultures of you are only as important as the number of staff that report to you did not wash with me and I would not go down that route.

I insisted that I wanted to know the profitability of each component part of the group together with a consolidated set of accounts by the 20th of each month. This had much more significance to me than if one car was costing more than another or of how much we were spending on paper clips.

Tony agreed that this would be achievable and on this basis monthly board meetings were set for this date, when the figures could be perused and any changes in policy or direction made. However, he was still mumbling on about needing more help and would not accept my argument that he must reduce his analysis of minute detail, which would not have any significant effect on decision making and on that basis it had little or no value.

The effect of the competitive battle between Selkirk and Rite Vent was making John Hornby's sales targets more difficult to achieve, particularly in the Midland Area, bearing in mind my arrangement with Kevin Samuels. John would also be aware that Selkirk would eventually overcome their production problems with their flexible flue liner, which would present another obstacle to his sales targets. With these things in mind, and after discussion with Terry, I offered John the opportunity to return, in the capacity of MMF sales director, after eleven years away.

The chance for John to build a sales team that would be positioned to sell Selkirk, Rite Vent and the full range of MMF's own of stainless steel and Proheat products across the whole of the country, for what was now the largest distributor of flue products in the UK, was much too good an opportunity to turn down. I agreed a remuneration package with John and he rejoined MMF in May 1997. He quickly recruited Geoff Little, a Rite Vent salesman, to serve the Bristol office and cover the whole of the South West and Paul Bastable who was now a permanent sales fixture in the Midlands ploughed on relentlessly. He also later recruited Dave Huggins, another Rite Vent salesman, to cover the North West area of the country for MMF.

John, armed with the detailed sales reports from the Castle computer software, quickly drew up sales targets, detailed by product range, which would indicate what products were selling in which areas and within weeks the whole company was buzzing with new enthusiasm, the only long face belonged to sulking Tony Beard.

The clash that had been brewing finally came to a head before the move to Woodburn Road was completed. On reaching the office one Thursday morning, Tony had obviously been working himself into a frenzy on his way to the office, as he stormed into my office with his letter of resignation giving me the ultimatum that unless he was allowed to recruit an assistant, he was off. I did not open the letter and asked Tony to go home and not come back until Monday morning, giving him an opportunity to cool down and reconsider his decision.

Before Tony left the building, he discussed the implications of his departure with both Terry and John, advising them that the systems that he had now put in place were so complex and individual to him that he was indispensable. He told them that I would be begging for him to come back within a week. Terry, who could recall his experience when all of the fitting staff resigned on mass and John who had known me for much longer than Tony, both told him in no uncertain terms, not to try or even consider the possibility of this happening unless he really wanted to leave anyway.

Monday morning arrived together with a red faced Tony, in the same angered state and it was quite obvious that his position was unchanged I said quite calmly 'Tony, if you do not want to work for me I can't force you to.' and with that accepted his resignation. He left seven days later after having given only one weeks notice and without providing very much help to me about his personalised unique accounting systems, but not before I had repurchased his shares for £5000, the same shares that I had given to Tony as a loyalty bonus a few years before. The repurchasing of the shares was to have great significance for me a few years later, but at the time I believed that I was merely performing a tidying up exercise.

Tony may have had second thoughts about the way he was leaving the company, or had other motives, he told me if I had any problems, don't hesitate to give him a call. I had an inkling that Tony wanted to start his own accounting company and believed that he would get the

MMF accounting work on a sub contract basis. If this was the case, he certainly went the wrong way about it, but the £5000 he received for the shares, would probably have been a big help to him in a start up situation.

I may have been calm on the surface, but I was under no illusion about the amount of time and work that would be needed to restore the efficient way the accounts had been produced throughout Tony's tenure. My belief that the tail should never wag the dog was paramount in accepting Tony's resignation; I had managed without an accountant before and I would manage without an accountant again.

In order to fully understand Tony's systems, I set about the forensic analysis of his spreadsheets, under the added pressure that the annual audit was looming, but I was determined not to find myself in this situation again. In future I would know better than any accountant the intricacies of the accounting system. Working by day, well into the night and tirelessly over the Christmas break, I had mastered how the computer had been set for automatic postings and once all of the spreadsheets had been dissected and reassembled into a form that I could easily follow, I realised what a fantastic system I had inherited. I had occasion just after Christmas to telephone Tony about a minor detail of which I was unsure, which Tony could have given an answer to straight away to see how his offer of help stood up. Tony offered to come in on a *fee basis* to sort that and any other problems for the audit, I was disappointed with his response and I declined his offer, replaced the receiver, and never spoke to him again.

Tony's exit brought the return of Joan, in my current state of thinking an infinitely better exchange. Her return came about after a serious fall off a ladder in the kitchen and she fractured one of her vertebrae and although she made a complete recovery, lifting patients was out of the question and she had to give up nursing. She could see that Tony's departure had created a great deal of stress and had put pressure on me and she instantly volunteered to step into the breach again. The arrangement worked very well Joan looked after the whole of the purchase ledger side, Joanne carried out all of the sales ledger postings, cash chasing and credit control. Terry had always done the wages and within six months of Tony's departure, I was producing all of the accounts that had been required of an accountant and playing golf twice a week, so much for needing an assistant. All of the figures would be analysed at the monthly board meetings, comparing the actual sales against budgets and profitability of each faction of the company noted.

We now felt free to resurrect a two week touring holiday to Scotland and the Western Isles that had to be cancelled the previous year due to Joan's back injury. We chose to travel via the Lake District stopping over night, before travelling on to Oban to begin island hopping through Barr, South and North Uist taking in Harris and Lewis all via Caledonian MacBrayne ferries and soaking up the scenery. The Scottish landscape matched up to the Kerry scenery in equal measure with its lakes, hills and peat banks all adorned with grazing sheep. We both agreed and were disappointed that in general the Scottish welcome fell short of what we were used to in Ireland and contrasted somewhat with the glorious and spectacular scenery.

We returned home to learn of the tragic death of Princess Diana, caused by a road accident in Paris The television coverage of the funeral, which followed on the 6th of September stunned the nation, as the gun carriage left Kensington Palace followed by two young grieving sons Harry and William following along the funeral route lined by over a million people, all providing a cavalcade of floral tributes, being affectionately tossed towards the coffin on its journey to Westminster Abbey.

Other things were also happening in my life at this time. I had been a member of the Catenian Association since 1982. Catenian membership is restricted to practising male Catholics, who have a business or professional background. Having served as Vice President of the Streetly Circle throughout 1995, I was elected to be President in April 1996. It was a special year, in that it encompassed the celebration of the circle's 250th meeting, a meeting which became a grand occasion having Bishop Pargeter as the guest of honour and the Grand Director Jim Quinn KCHS LLB proposing the toast to the circle, to which I responded on behalf of the Streetly members.

An annual occasion in the presidential year was the President's Mass, which is entirely the presidents' responsibility as to the form that the day would take. I had arranged for the Mass to be held in a tiny church built by the Thogmorton's in 1825, in the grounds of Harvington Hall. The Mass was followed by dinner in Harvington Hall, a mediaeval moated Manor House built in the 1580s and truly a historical setting for a special occasion. It was a very busy year of office, as I visited all twenty five circles in province six and as many ladies' informal nights that I could fit in to the schedule so that my years' visiting around the Province was spent with Joan whenever possible.

It was a very full year on all fronts as the volume of business that MMF was generating with Selkirk products, at this time was well in excess of a million pounds per annum. An invitation arrived for Joan and me to be guests of Selkirk for four days cruising on the QE2. We gratefully accepted the invitation and when the time came, we decided to extend the holiday by travelling to Devon a few days early, spending time visiting Salcombe and Plymouth Hoe, before meeting up with the other Selkirk guests in Southampton to board the QE2. No one could ever say that Selkirk did anything by halves; we were entertained while waiting to board and on arrival in our cabin, Selkirk monogrammed towels were waiting on the bed, together with a detailed itinerary for the four days, staring with cocktails before dinner.

The QE2 sailed the first leg of the cruise to Le Havre, to have our arrival met by several fire boats, cascading their hoses and flares flashing into the sky a truly spectacular welcome. There were always cocktails before dinner and this led to an amusing incident when a mix up occurred with the drinks. Joan had ordered an orange juice and after taking it off the tray, thought it tasted unusual, but said nothing. Only a few minutes later, one of the other ladies complained that her Screwdriver only tasted like orange Juice. Joan had taken to the booze without knowing, but discreetly left most of it on the table when she left to enjoy the evening entertainment.

On the third morning, we had been told not to have breakfast. The QE2 had sailed from Le Havre and was moored in Cove and tenders would take us ashore, to be met by a coach driver, who could have been a comedian in the West End and to everyone's amusement conveyed us to a full traditional Irish breakfast, at the Jameson Distillery, in Middleton, County Cork. Whiskey tasting followed a tour of the distillery and I had to drink Joan's as usual, a cross I always bore willingly, because despite my infatuation with business and my eccentricities, I never drove Joan to drink, except by default. We left Joan's home county and returned with the Irish comedian to the QE2 and more cocktails, dinner and a further first rate variety show hosted by an Irish comedian, while cruising back to Southampton and to the end of an immensely enjoyable break, spent with good friends and great company.

With the move to Woodburn Road complete and the retirement of Mervin Wright, John's arrival had given the company a new growth spurt. The debt with Selkirk and Rite Vent had been discharged, the pension fund was growing annually, the bank was in the black for most of each month and my thoughts were beginning to lead to further expansion plans as ten years had elapsed since the purchase of Proheat.

Michelle had returned home with Michael in February 1996 and both found employment quickly, Michelle at Sandwell Hospital for a short spell, before securing a post in Accident and Emergency at Good Hope Hospital in Sutton Coldfield. Joan was delighted to have another one of her beloved daughters back home in the fold.

But Claire's diabetic condition was starting to cause some additional health problems and regular hospital appointments became more frequent. An appointment was made for her to be seen by a professor of gastroenterology at St. Marks Hospital at Harrow. St. Mark's was a centre of excellence for gastric problems and although she stayed there for two weeks, even celebrating her 24th birthday on the ward, she only saw the professor once and except for the first hearing the words 'Autonomic Neuropathy', little seemed to come from these consultations, which was possibly a case of a specialist in one field not recognising the complications in a zone outside of his own area of expertise.

Sometime later her consultant at the Manor Hospital in Walsall, Dr. Cox, agreed to replace the nasal gastric feed, which was cosmetically embarrassing to Claire, with a gastric peg feed to be fitted directly into her stomach, but this operation went badly wrong and resulted in peritonitis and a spell in intensive care. Our eyes were glued to the monitors for three days before the danger had passed and she could be fed with concentrated high vitamin fluids being pumped into her stomach, usually at night, through the peg feeding tube.

Selkirk's generosity was repeated the following year with an invitation for Joan and I to go, for men's semi finals day at Wimbledon. I was to find out later that this had caused quite a tantrum with Mike Moran, when he found out that the cost for this one day was greater than the cruise the previous year. The cost for tickets for seats ten rows from the Royal Box, champagne reception, followed by lunch and a strawberry and cream tea was £3000 per head. He had tried to cancel the promotion, but without success and in rage had offered to pass the tickets on to the Salvation Army, only to be told 'There is a dress code Sir.' which did nothing for his health or temper.

We travelled to London the night before by train and checked into a hotel near Victoria Station, as we had booked to see Starlight Express that evening. The following morning we met up at another hotel with David Jones, who arrived late, after being held up by a train derailment near Temple Meads station. We were then taken by limousine to SW1 and the spectacular Wimbledon complex for an experience of a lifetime. The whole atmosphere on the Centre Court was as stimulating as being on the Kop at Anfield, but much more comfortable, dignified and refined.

This was to be Dave Jones and Mike Moran's swan song, as the substantial profit history that John Botton had generated for many years had quickly eluded Mike. Dave Jones was continually frustrated, by what he saw as manic decisions, made by a man with little or no experience in the nuances of the flue business and without the wisdom to take advice. After a bad weekend, David drove to the Barnstaple office fuming and on arrival, David met with Mike Moran and a blazing row exploded, which resulted in David's instant dismissal. With a gagging clause that would have affected his severance package if it had been breached and I am not able to record all of the background to this situation. I had great sympathy with David and visited him at home to offer any support that I could give.

But regardless of what was happening at Selkirk, my thoughts of expansion returned and I believed that the time was now right and sufficient funds were available for a new branch to be opened, the first for a decade. I was first attracted to the South of England as I believed that this would be most desirable location and spent two days in and around the Southampton area looking at properties, only to find that there was not a great deal available and premises that were offered by agents were expensive and came with high rateable values. It was also an area of full employment which may have driven salaries higher than in other branches. Starting a new branch with high overheads would have extended the period before it became profitable and I decided that this was not the best route to expand the company.

I returned to Woodburn Road disappointed, but made further enquiries with both Selkirk and Rite Vent, as to where they thought that their distribution would most benefit from a new depot, and to my surprise they both opted for the North East.

With this in mind I contacted commercial property agents in Newcastle, Gateshead and Darlington and travelled up the M1/A1 full of enthusiasm and went on to make an offer of £130,000 for the first suitable property in Gateshead, but that offer was rejected.

The Agent suggested another property within sight of the A1 at Swalwell in Gateshead. It was an impressive building, with good access more than ample offices and all of the warehouse racking was part of the deal, I again offered £130,000 to a filtration distributor, which equalled my offer for the other premises that were less suitable and this offer was accepted.

The solicitor's searches found that the building had been constructed at the top of a deep mine shaft, but the Coal Board gave guarantees that it had been structurally sealed correctly and the purchase went ahead. I recruited Adrian Wood from Rite Vent to manage the branch and he had no trouble in employing a driver and warehouseman, as unemployment was high in the area, which had seen the decline in both the mining and shipbuilding industries. Adrian was well known to me from my dealings with the Rite Vent sales office. Stocking deals were again negotiated with the main suppliers and

MMF North Eastern branch was up and running and even greater ties were being cemented with Rite Vent, whose factory was only a few miles up the motorway in Washington. MMF was also finding it difficult to get any help from Derek Preston the Selkirk area sales manager, as his loyalties lay firmly with Docherty's who had a branch in Leeds.

While the Rite Vent relationship with me was improving, Selkirk was moving in the opposite direction, when Mike Moran's position at Selkirk was to be short lived and he was replaced by Chris Borkett, who turned out to be an even bigger disaster for MMF, and it was rumoured that he had connections with 3i's and had been put into Selkirk to prepare a management buy out.

Chris was a man of medium height and neat in appearance, but a personality which exuded with his own importance and he made some very curious appointments. Alan Shelton, a paint salesman was given the role of international sales director, Mike Hodgson a retired logistics Army Colonel, became operations director, to most people in the trade he was referred to as Colonel Bogy, especially as service plummeted to all time depths with hardly a single delivery ever being made either complete, correct or on time. A very efficient production and transport system was destroyed almost over night by a reorganisation that became a disaster, which no amount of meetings or complaints could rectify. The only sensible addition to the board was Frank Carter who was a long standing Selkirk employee and who had had vast experience in contracting and especially large chimney and flue installations.

In an effort to pacify a rebellious and disenchanted distributor network, Chris Borkett, who was a keen sailor invited Joan and I, together with other distributors, onto an ocean going tall sailing ship for the finale of Cowes Week. On joining the ship we were warmly welcomed with champagne, a galactic array of delicious buffet food and wines to the accompaniment of waiters dancing in attendance. The firing of a cannon signified the start of the closing ceremony, which was concluded with a spectacular firework display. We returned to our hotel impressed by a very enjoyable evening, spent with many old friends.

CHAPTER SEVENTEEN

Wedding Bells

Michelle and Michael's relationship had been kept under good stewardship while living at home with us in Streetly and at last Michael popped the question and wedding plans were the order of the day with many visits to Wedding Fayres' most weekends. Penns Hall Hotel one weekend, the Belfry next, excitedly viewing everything from wedding dresses to cake designs.

Joan was thrilled with the opportunity to help with the wedding arrangements and planning for the event, which was to take place in Millstreet on 14th May 1999. Another wedding that was to follow our footsteps thirty six years before in St. Patrick's Church, Michelle's wedding strategy was more like a military operation as she was quite certain what she wanted and how it would all fit together. Early planning for the Irish wedding was essential in Michelle's mind. She planned a trip to Ireland to view venues and make bookings, but Joan, who was never a great sailor or traveller had decided against a weekend trip. The Swansea to Cork ferry was booked, together with cabins for the ten-hour crossing and Michelle, Claire and I set off by road on the well worn route to the Swansea ferry for the weekend, with an array of ideas in mind, but Claire's deteriorating health was to play its part. A worrying situation occurred on the crossing, when at 6.00am in the morning, Michelle tried to wake Claire in the cabin, she would not stir, she was in a coma and showing signs of fitting.

She called me in the next cabin and we searched Claire's bag for a blood sugar testing kit, without success and as mentioned earlier Claire had been experiencing digestive problems and her nutrition was being supplemented by peg feeding, with the tube in her stomach. I left Michelle to care for Claire, and I raced around the ship in search of sugar and warm water and asked the Purser to put out a call for a doctor and any diabetic on board with a testing kit to go to cabin 316. I hurried back to the cabin and asked Michelle to start trying to pour the sugar water solution into the peg feed. It was a very hit and miss method of trying to get this sugar solution into the tube, but finally a doctor arrived along with a testing kit. The testing kit indicated a 'Lo' sugar count, so we knew that we were doing the right thing in trying to get sugar into the system. The doctor confirmed this, but could not give much further help, as he did not have a Glucagon injection with him. The ferry crew arranged for an ambulance to be waiting at the ferry port in Cork and immediately after docking, Michelle travelled with Claire in the ambulance to the Regional Hospital, as it was known then and I drove the car off the ferry and followed behind to the hospital.

Michelle said that Claire had stared to recover consciousness in the ambulance and by the time I arrived, Claire was sitting up with sweet tea and eating toast. That was the end of Claire's wedding planning, much to her disgust she had to stay in hospital under observation, while Michelle and I went touring hotels to book the reception and after detailed inspections of at least five, Christy's in Blarney was chosen and booked.

The evening was taken up visiting Claire in hospital, who was very frustrated that she was missing out on her holiday break and the wedding planning. After visiting time was over we stopped for an overdue meal at Dan Sheahan's, a pub in Ovens beyond Ballincolig, before returning to the bungalow tired but pleased with our days work.

The Church had already been booked and Michelle wanted to follow our footsteps in Millstreet Parish Church, where Michael would have grown up attending the Sunday Mass ritual. The following day Michelle had made an appointment to meet Maria Cassidy, a harpist and vocalist that she had heard about and who lived in Killarney. When we met Maria she played the harp and sang like an angel, in the front room of her home, almost everything that was requested she just reeled out: Panis Angelicus, Ave Maria and many more.

After much consideration and suggestions from Maria we chose the music selection and notes were made for the order of service and another booking had been completed. Incidentally Maria Cassidy is the mother of Jessica who auditioned on TV for 'I'd do anything' the Lloyd Webber musical, losing narrowly in the final.

We returned to see Claire again in hospital to find that she could be discharged the next day, which was quite a blessing, as we were due to return on the 9.00pm crossing the following evening. Michelle already had names and telephone numbers for bands and discos, which she had heard at other weddings and would enable her to book them by telephone. After a good night's sleep and an early breakfast with mission accomplished, we collected Claire from the hospital and were much more mindful of her on the return ferry journey, which was uneventful.

A great deal more planning was underway on our return, which was more in Mum's domain: wedding dress, tiara and shoes had to be just right, bridesmaid dresses had to be agreed with Claire and Kate, Joan's outfit could not clash with the groom's mother's outfit, invitations printed and posted, all had to be completed before Joan and I set sail into the sunset, to give our second eldest daughter away.

In Ireland, the final phase of planning was underway, with guests travelling from England. Accommodation and travel had to be booked for the visitors, this in itself was difficult as the The Wallis Arms Hotel in Millstreet did not cater for residents at that time and the nearest hotel was The Isle of Sky Hotel which was not very salubrious either. Joan was busy with Michelle, sorting out flowers for the church and buttonholes for the main participants, while the men were being fitted for morning suits. We made a joint effort in organising a buffet reception in the bungalow for the visitors from England and close relatives on the eve of the wedding. John Husband and wife Anna lost their way on the journey down from Dublin after heading for the wrong Millstreet, but despite John's notoriously inept navigational skills, the big day finally came. Joanne was maid of honour, Claire, although very weak, was fit and determined to join Kate as Michelle's bridesmaid. Jack was pageboy taking his responsibility for the rings very seriously, until he fell asleep in the church and Katie Rogers, looking like a little angel, was the flower girl. A Vintage Sunbeam Talbot car arrived at the bungalow, on a cool but bright May morning, to collect the radiant Bride and me, the proud father.

The Church looked magnificent, the alter adorned with specially chosen flowers, and the angelic music reverberating throughout the church from Maria Cassidy's harp, accompanied by the sweet tones from a powerful contralto voice, resonating amid perfect acoustics, that held the congregation speechless as they listened to this feast of musical magic. Michelle and I started the long walk up the aisle to signal the beginning of Maria's rendering of the Wedding March, and the formal start of the Nuptial Mass. Cannon Manning had chosen to perform the ceremony himself and this caused some consternation when he decided to ignore the order of service, which had been composed and published after considerable care by Michelle and his deviations left the non Catholics floundering as to where they were in the ceremony.

After the signing of the register and many photographs, the convoy of cars with horns blaring and lights flashing, made its way to the six hundred year old Blarney Castle, famous for the kissing stone. Most of the guests made their way to Christy's for the pre-dinner Sherry or Champagne, while a marathon photo shoot was taken in the Castle grounds before the Bride and Groom rejoined their guests.

Christy's banqueting room was an ideal setting, with a large millwheel turning, the slow rotation generated by a flow of water that created a very calming atmosphere. Michelle, Michael and all of the top table guests were piped into the main reception by a lone Celtic Piper, which helped to set the tone for the feast selected by Michelle and Michael, after much discussion with Mum and me.

The telegrams were read and I welcomed Michael into the family commenting that when he moved in to his own house, I would get my parking spot back on the drive and other speeches at times moving, particularly Michael's, when he paid tribute to his mother, as he had lost his father when he was very small and she had struggled to rear him and four other children single handed.

After a short break the band swung into action and within minutes, the floor was bouncing to the beat and the lead singer managed to get everyone on the floor. The fluency of the music kept the ballroom packed, there was a pause for a short interval when Mike's school friends gave their own vocal interlude of what would be best described as Irish rugby songs, Don Twomey gave his usual rendition of a few Rebel Songs, before the real talent took control of the music again. The band completed their performance at midnight, to make way for the disco, which raised the tempo to an even higher pitch, before Michelle, who had hardly left the floor all night, almost collapsed in a happy state of exhaustion. The great day was over; the Bride and Groom were on their way to a Caribbean Cruise. After a short holiday Joan, Claire and I returned home to see what I would get up to next.

Joan's great love was her garden, it's true to say *her* garden, because I had little interest in her main hobby, but I did take great pride in seeing her creations, as each flower bed was nurtured to give colour for most of the year. Sunday outings would often be to garden centres, to buy plants or bird tables, in fact anything to enhance the spectacle from the kitchen or conservatory windows. Granddaughter Katie spent a very enjoyable summer holiday before she started school helping in the garden with her Nan, finding worms and snails, while digging with her own little hand fork and being spoilt by Joan.

CHAPTER EIGHTEEN

End of an Era

Totally out of the blue I received a telephone call from John Dalkin, a senior executive at BSS plc, a publicly quoted company and well known in the heating industry John was a man I had met earlier in the John Macatta era, and he enquired, 'Could he make an appointment to revisit some of the earlier talks?' He was employed by BSS to seek possible acquisitions and had obviously followed MMF's profit growth from figures lodged at Companies House and was interested to know if MMF could be acquired by the BSS Group. I confirmed that it could, if the price was right. A meeting was arranged and a tall man in his late fifties with an easy relaxed style arrived at the MMF offices and introduced himself as John Dalkin. The meeting continued with discussions about synergy and the BSS ambitious expansion plans concluded with agreement that a further meeting would follow. Two weeks later, a private room in The Post House Hotel, Great Barr, was booked and I provided John with a copy of the latest accounts and went on to discuss how the proposed acquisition would affect the existing employees and myself, post takeover. I was comfortable with what I heard and at the next meeting

John produced a letter of intent and letters of confidentiality were exchanged at the subsequent meeting.

I agreed that I would sell the company for a price that was based on a PE of five, which was about the right ratio for a private company in that sector. Joan was quite disappointed and a little upset that a lifetime of nostalgic memories and a rollercoaster ride of successes and failures that the last twenty five years had brought, might pass out of our control. She saw it as my life time of work, but I had always worked to build the business for a sale, at some point in time and at sixty years of age a decade more than I had initially planned, I believed that now was the right time and as subsequent health problems turned out, the timing could not have been better.

At John Dalkin's request, I arranged for visits to all of the branches on the pretext of insurance inspections. Terry was the only other shareholder who was aware of what may happen, but outside of me, Joan and Terry, it was strictly confidential, due to BSS being a publicly quoted company. The stock exchange would have to be informed when a formal offer was made. Negotiations had reached an advanced stage after a meeting with the BSS managing director and indications that the letter of intent would be replaced by a formal written offer but nothing happened after that meeting. After two weeks had elapsed, I telephoned John for an explanation, he apologised and explained that a much bigger acquisition had arisen, which he could not expand upon due to confidentially commitments, I was assured that there was no problem, BSS would definitely go ahead with the acquisition, but there would be a delay.

Several months elapsed, with more assurances and apologies from BSS that the other acquisition was taking longer than expected, but they would move forward, as soon as it had been completed. But I was feeling more and more annoyed that I was being sidelined and getting anxious when I received a telephone call from Ken Elrick, who had been tipped off by Mike Rudd, a friend and fellow Catenian and head of MMF's firm of auditors, that I may be looking for a buyer.

Ken explained what he had to offer and a meeting was arranged at his home in Worcester. I arrived at his house and met a man of medium height with a rotund figure, in his mid fifties with a confident aura of experience about him. I quickly expressed my reservations, which were founded on the Macatta saga of old, but Ken reassured me that there was no retainer and no fees until and unless a sale had been completed. On this basis I had nothing to lose so I provided him with copies of the last five years' accounts and advised him of the BSS offer on the table, which would not earn him any fee if it went through.

Ken made his living from selling and merging companies and was very well connected with a number of Venture Capital Houses, who were willing to back prospective management buy outs or management buy in teams and within a week he had put me in touch with a Mr. Tullow, a single guy whose background was in retail management and had capital to invest if the right opportunity presented itself, but he was quickly discarded as a nit picking time waster. Another introduction followed from a group of three individuals with experience of the building materials industry and had financial backing from 3is.

An initial meeting was set up at the Sutton Court Hotel and following discussions about the synergy of their experience and the reasons for my desire to sell, the buy in trio was headed up by a Welsh man Dave Thomas. His nationality was not a good starting point in my eyes, but letters of confidentiality were exchanged, with me agreeing that Ken could forward all of the historical accounts to them. Ken knew he was working against the clock as BSS may return to the table at any time and was eager to push a deal through with all haste.

I warmed to Dave Thomas, the leader of the trio, who came across as a no nonsense, let's get on with it attitude, after having exchanged financial information with 3is and their bankers, he made a substantially better offer to buy the business, on the basis that I would repurchase the Woodburn Road premises and lease it back to the buy in company. I was also happier that this group would move the company forward, in much the way I had driven it, whereas the BSS offer may have caused some reorganisation difficulties for the loyal and in many cases long serving employees.

Ken recommended that I should employ Richard Knight of Rickerby Watterson in Cheltenham to carry out the legal work, as he had achieved several acquisitions for Ken in the past, very efficiently and a fee of £21,000 was agreed for the legal work, which was to start with immediate effect.

There was an enormous amount of legal work involved. In addition to the sale contract itself there was all of the property to deal with, which was Ed Mosley's province, plus my ongoing contract and the purchase and lease back of the Woodburn Road property, all with the buyers, 3is and the Bank of Scotland, who were all financing the purchase. Due diligence was completed by an independent firm of accountants, who charged a huge fee to the purchasers for a very inadequate job and produced a laughable report, which did nothing for my opinion of accountants. In addition independent property valuations were carried out at all locations.

There had been several hiccups along the way. In fact I had told Ken Elrick one Friday evening, after the lease back deal on the premises was shorter in duration than I wanted that the deal was off, but Ken persuaded me to sleep on it over the weekend, and not to make any decision until Monday morning. After discussions with Joan, who was now getting tired and stressed with the on off situations, I backed down and the deal was back on.

There was a pause in all of the legal wheeling and dealing, as the much awaited Millennium Celebrations were underway, with parties and fireworks all having a greater significance than in previous years. Television pictures began arriving early morning and throughout the day from across the world, as the Millennium arrived firstly in Australia working its way across the time lines of the globe to the UK. The worries that Y2K would also cause mayhem with computerised technology drifted into oblivion, as everyone returned to work wondering what the 21st century would bring.

The deal was very close to completion when John Dalkin telephoned confirming that he was now able to disclose that BSS had fully acquired PTS, a large and well known group of builders' merchants and was now in a position to proceed with the MMF purchases. This caused me some consternation, as it was now time for me to start stalling as I really wanted the current deal to reach a conclusion, but thought it wise to keep my options open in case the buy in crowd threw any last minute spanners in the works, causing it to fall through. I told John of BSS that I would be in Ireland for two weeks and I would telephone him on my return, which gave extra time to ensure the completion with the buy in trio.

Finally on the 29th March 2000 a completion meeting was arranged, surprisingly nearly a hundred miles apart with Joan and I meeting with our team in the opulent Cheltenham solicitor's office and the purchasing team, which included Terry McIvor and John Hornby, who were to become directors and shareholders of the newly bought company, together with all their professional advisors, all gathered at Grant Thornton offices in London.

We were told that we need not arrive at the Rickerby Watterson offices until two o'clock, as there would be many preliminary exchanges between opposing solicitors, before they got down to the nitty gritty of finalisation of details, or the signing of the contracts. The exchanges of minor detail went on and on, to and fro between London and Cheltenham, before we finally signed the completion deal at eight thirty that evening.

The Company that I had founded and nurtured and watched develop over the past twenty five years and had grown from an annual turnover of zero to 5.5 million pounds, in which time I had opened three additional branches and made two acquisitions had now finally passed into new ownership.

We invited our legal team and Ken Elrick to a celebration dinner in Cheltenham, only to find that when the bill was presented, I did not have my credit card with me and Joan who was better prepared, settled the bill with her credit card. Joan very soberly, drove both millionaires home. I who had consumed more of the Champagne and wine than anyone else and was without doubt a little merry retiring to bed, but happy with the deal and content that all of my years of sweat and toil had been crystallised into cash.

Regardless of the sale proceeds, the very substantial pension fund, plus the rental income from the Woodburn Road property, together with the Alma Street properties would enable us to live very comfortably for the rest of our lives. Whilst this would not be a huge sum of money to many, to that little boy from 2 back of 312 Cooksey Road, that had been bottom of his class at school, it was!

The newly found wealth meant nothing at all to Joan but she was very proud of the man she had married thirty five years earlier and pleased that we would be able to spend more time together.

The Alma Street premises, which were outside of the company sale deal, were eventually sold and although there was only a marginal profit on the sale, the rental income that had been generated had made a useful contribution both personally and to the pension fund.

The buy in team had formed a new company Tremilo, as a holding company to purchase MMF and I had a year-long contract to continue working for them to ensure a smooth hand over to the new owners. One of the few times that I was called upon to help was when Chris Borkett Selkirk CEO, issued a summons for David Thomas and his team to meet at their offices in Barnstaple. David, now MD, together with John Hornby, sales director and me, now only acting in a consultancy capacity, arrived to face what can only be described as a cross between the Last Supper and a Parliamentary Select committee meeting.

Over the years, I had visited the Barnstaple factory on many occasions and always been welcomed by smiling faces and an almost unique Selkirk hospitality, but on this occasion, together with David and John we found ourselves seated facing a horseshoe of inquisitors. Borkett played the part of Pontius Pilate, with Rob Dolby, financial director, and Frank Carter on his left, Colonel Bogey and Shelton on his right, his director of Human Resources, the works manager, the sales office manager, the canteen manager, and the car park attendant were all the inquisitors. What plans did the new management of MMF have for the future? The canteen manager and car park attendant is a bit of poetic licence, but the orchestration of this event was so over the top, that it calls for some scorn.

The whole scenario was such a farce that it could have been dreamed up by Brian Rix. Chris Borkett was making a complete idiot of himself and displaying so many of his inadequacies in having to have his whole Board of Directors plus extras to handle what should have been a meeting of like-minded people, that David could not resist saying that he did not believe that it was any business of Mr. Borkett what his plans were, and was about to leave and take his colleagues with him.

Frank Carter calmed the situation down by saying that they only wanted assurances that the two companies would continue to work closely together, as they had done in the past. I confirmed the obvious; that both companies would need each other in the future, just as much as they had in the past and what would change. What advantage could possibly be gained by changing the direction of a successful company? Chris Borkett must have thought that he had displayed enough of his power to his minions and the meeting broke up amicably with Chris Borkett inviting everyone to dinner, which was small recompense for a waste of so many executives' time.

A totally different situation arose when we travelled to Washington to make our introductions to the Rite Vent directors, where we all received a very warm welcome with a grand tour of the factory. We had all been booked into the Post House Hotel and were later collected and wined and dined at a very exclusive restaurant and all was going very well, until Ken Thompson, the newly appointed sales director, who obviously was going through some mid life crisis, suggested that they carry on to a night club. At his urging, two sixty year olds and a forty something year old David, all piled into a taxi and wound up in a fairly remote late night drinking bar, adorned with an adequate supply of women, who could most politely be described as hostesses. Ken made a beeline for one female who he obviously knew well, whom he proceeded to wrap himself around to the embarrassment of all of the MMF personnel, who could not get out of the place quick enough, with all of the good work in courting the new owners wasted by a serious misjudgement.

However, after these two fiascos and with the introductions to the main suppliers complete I felt that the new team had their own plans and agenda and was a little disappointed that I felt in the way, as they had not called on my years of experience to any great extent. I had kept all of the accounts tidy as far as I was able, but the factoring arrangement with the Bank of Scotland and the new director's personal fanatical arrangements were kept confidential to themselves, I believed that the time was right to gradually drift away from Woodburn Road, but I was at the end of the telephone if any queries arose. Joanne stayed on with the new team, becoming an integral member looking after the sales ledger and credit control for all branches. I had many plans of my own and was keen to move on to a new chapter of my life, with more flexibility while pursuing new ideas.

CHAPTER NINETEEN

JMCK Properties

The sale of MMF was the end of an engineering chapter in my life, but another was about to begin in property. JMCK Properties Ltd. takes its title from the first initial of the names of each of my four daughters and was formed to buy the Woodburn Road property from MMF. The purchase was completed as part of the original deal and the property was to be leased back to MMF's new owners on a lease of twenty-year duration, with rent reviews and break clauses every five years. It was a deal that was to turn out very favourably when JMCK sold the property nearly five years later, for nearly double the purchase price and after collecting most of the original value of the property in rental income. Maybe I did have a Midas touch after all.

Ken Elrick, who had engineered the sale of MMF, recommended that I make contact with David Gear, who was the managing director of Robinson Gear, a firm with an unblemished reputation for pension and investment advice. I telephoned David and arranged a meeting in their offices on the Hagley Road. David was obviously a very astute man of small stature with a very polished and neat appearance. The meeting, which Joan also attended, turned out to be very productive, both in reorganising the pension fund investment and also with investments that would minimise the capital gains tax liability from the sale of the company.

Michael and Michelle had purchased a house in Kings Road, New Oscott and Michelle had returned to work in A & E at Good Hope Hospital, when she broke the news that she was expecting her first baby and a third grandchild for us, we were overjoyed that we had another great event to look forward to, which duly occurred with the arrival of Andrew Thomas Smyth on 1st November 2000.

A further property was purchased in Thornhill Road for development, but only as a hobby and not an addiction, as MMF had been. The purchase had been inspired by the break up of Joanne's marriage and the deterioration in Claire's health. Mountain Greenery Nursing Home just around the corner in Thornhill Road was for sale. I surveyed the property, with a view to converting it into three self-contained flats and after seeking professional advice, I created a Discretionary Trust in favour of my daughters and the Trust purchased the Mountain Greenery property. The objective was to provide a two bedroom flat for Joanne, Jack and Katie, a one bedroom flat for Claire to give her a degree of independence, while both would be close enough to us if they needed our support. Together with a two bedroom apartment, which could be leased and thus provide income for all of the girls within the Trust.

I drew up my own plans and initially had two skiving council workmen helping me with the project, but I quickly saw that this would not work out and as they say in Ireland, I gave them the road. This was to lead to a great friendship that still lives on today. It was brought about through a fellow Catenian and golfing friend Chris Langan, who introduced me to Ron Gerrard, a retired tool maker, who spent most of his spare time doing all manner of carpentry work and toy making in his garage. I asked Ron, who had limited vision and deteriorating eyesight, if he would work with me on the conversion, remuneration was agreed and we decided that we would spend three days each week on the Thornhill Road project.

Ron was unable to drive due to his impaired vision and I would collect him on work days at 8.00 am and after a morning's toil, Joan would bring sandwiches, pork pies and make tea for lunch, which we all enjoyed together and Joan would prepare dinner with a beer and a glass of wine for 6.00pm, before returning Ron to his home, tired and happy with the success of the day's progress.

Our combined experience, coupled with a few mistakes, and amid great camaraderie, partition walls were demolished, others added, plastering, plumbing, heating, re wiring, painting and decorating, the ground floor was completed within a few months. The total project was not to be completed for a further year, but a lasting friendship was forged and grew as our achievements came to fruition and Ron became part of the family sharing Joanne's and particularly Claire's aspirations.

We organised a grand opening party to celebrate the completion of the ground floor, which coincided with Andrew Smyth's Christening on 9th December 2000. Many of Michelle and Michael's relatives came from Ireland, Kate who was Andrew's Godmother, with her husband Donal and many friends and relations all enjoyed good food and all manner of beverages. A great day was nearing its conclusion late into the night, when Ron, sitting in the newly constructed dining area, gracefully slid off the chair, with a smile on his face, descending under the table into alcoholic oblivion. It must be said in his defence that Marie, Michael's sister had been topping up both his and the neighbour, Tom Hawley's whiskey glasses most of the evening.

We had decorated both of the ground floor flats to the individual occupant's requirements and Joanne, Jack and Katie moved into their apartment on the left of the entrance with all of their furniture from Minstead Road, where the house had been sold reasonably quickly for a small profit for Joanne. Claire used some of her savings to buy new furniture and took great delight in feathering her little nest to suit her own requirements. But we were becoming more and more concerned about Claire's health, which was causing her ongoing problems, she had reduced her hours at the Cottage Hospital and was only able to work part time when she felt well enough.

The following summer Jack and Katie joined Claire and all the family except Joanne, when we travelled to Ireland for our annual holiday, which took its usual form, trips to the Blasket and Sherkin islands, the Zoo at Fota Island and all of the children having great fun together with their cousins. I would take a few drinks down in Lal's Bar with Joan's brother and sister, Dennis and Nora.

We returned home to England after a welcome break from our continuing toils on the 108 Project to a surprise, to find that Joanne had a live in partner, Richard. This caused us a little consternation, in that

Joanne's inability to pick good friends at school and a husband that had left her with two small children, whom she had now divorced, did not bode well for this Richard character. To add to the problem, Joan's moral Catholic upbringing did not really countenance 'living together', which also brought worries about Jack and Katie's welfare, but they were soon dispelled as they got to know Richard better. Richard was a tall man of large proportions with a background in accountancy with a good job and a caring disposition.

Kate had completed her Business Studies degree in 1997 and was off to Ireland as quickly as her legs would take her, possibly Donal was an even bigger attraction than Ireland. She took up permanent residency in the bungalow and quickly secured a good job in Alps, where Michelle had previously worked. This was an idyllic situation for her, freedom from parental scrutiny with many friends in Ireland, the craic and Donal continued until 2001, when by coincideence both Kate and Donal found themselves unemployed at the same time, and decided that America was the place to be.

Equipped with ninety day visas Kate and Donal flew to Boston, which accommodated a large Irish community and quickly found work, Donal on a building site and Kate after sorting out an apartment was employed as a waitress come bar person. On the 11th of September after watching the Twin Towers collapse on the television I telephoned Kate to get her reaction. Due to the time gap, Kate was only just getting up and was totally unaware of the unfolding disaster. I told her that the terrorist planes had taken off from Logan International at Boston, the airport that we had booked to fly out to visit Kate and Donal. Three weeks later we landed at Logan International for a four-day tour of the city. We had previously had holidays in Texas and Florida, but we found Boston to have a much more English flavour about it and we enjoyed our short stay immensely, in spite of the increased airport security.

However, the disaster dashed any hopes of their staying beyond the limit of their visas and after visiting Donal's relation Fr. Paddy in Nebraska and a short holiday in Florida, paid for by their own American earned income, they returned to the bungalow in Ireland, where, after a short time Kate secured a very good post with Flextronics an International Electronics company in Cork, of which Caroline Dowling, a Millsreet woman was chief of European sales and Donal secured a lucrative precision engineering job, making hip and knee replacement parts.

My new found freedom led me to accept more invitations to travel on a number of golfing holidays with Catenian friends, twice to Florida and the most memorable to Palm Springs. I managed to sneak Ron Gerrard, my 108 Thornhill project cohort, into the party when someone dropped out at the last minute. The holidays were superbly organised by a friend, Frank Miller, who had flights arranged with Aer Lingus from Birmingham to Dublin, where we went through American immigration and then on to Los Angeles, with two hire vehicles booked for the drive from LA to Palm Springs.

The one slight hitch in the planning occurred when we arrived in Los Angeles at 5pm on a Friday evening, at the peak of the rush hour and negotiating our way along seven lane highways of compacted traffic, the two vehicles were inevitably split up, but fortunately Palm

Springs is only a very small town and we were soon re-united at the motel that had been pre-booked.

My golfing friends on this trip were John Husband who with his wife Anna had been long standing friends, Geoff Bannister, with whom I had had a time-honoured association, as a friend and with MMF, as he had done most of the art work for promotional literature, Frank Miller the organiser, Stan Leyland another Catenian and his brother in law Arthur and Ron Gerrard whose sight was now very poor, but came along for the craic.

Well the craic was mighty as they say in Ireland and the golf was unbelievable, as we enjoyed some of the best courses in the world, including Landmark the home of the multi million dollar skins competition, also Indian Springs and Desert Dunes all courses having lush manicured fairways carved out of the desert terrain, with many water features adding to the pleasure of playing golf in Californian sunshine.

I always had to have some project or challenge to drive me on and through JMCK I set myself the task of earning £25,000 in three months for the company. It was really an ego trip to see if I still had the capacity to earn £100K per annum, if I had to. JMCK bought a badly run down, repossessed house on the same estate where I had grown up, in Witton Lodge Road, a road that I would have travelled on my way to secondary school many years before. It was a three bedroom corner property, which meant that it was semi detached. It had obviously been on the market for a long time, as two agents' boards were found in the overgrown back garden, languishing amid weeds. The agent was asking for £95,000 and I offered £82,000, my offer was not unexpectedly rejected, but an increased offer of £87,000 on behalf of JMCK was accepted.

If the target was to be achieved my maximum budget of £13,000 was set for a total refurbishment which included adding a garage and upstairs shower and wash hand basin, the main bathroom being down stairs, re wiring, total redecoration, a new fireplace, carpets were fitted throughout and tidying up the garden. By carrying out much of the work myself, I stayed within budget, even after adding the legal fees. Three months later, with the help of two tradesmen, plus Ron Gerrard, who had helped me with the flat conversion and even Joanne and Richard gave a hand with the painting JMCK sold the renovated property to the first viewing family for £125,000, the limit of the stamp duty band and the target that I had set had been achieved.

Later that year, Joan received a letter inviting her to attend a routine mammogram check and within days she was recalled for an ultra sound scan and to have a biopsy taken. Having been a nurse she knew that this was serious and within days the bombshell exploded she had breast cancer and it was an aggressive tumour. The surgeon gave her the option of a lumpectomy or a mastectomy, but either way he would operate ten days later on 15th December. I insisted that we take no chances and to go for a total mastectomy, the priority in my mind was to get rid of the cancer. The specialist cancer nurses explained that the prospects of a full recovery were good and tried to give a devastated family reassurance, but we were all demented with worry.

With the top floor apartment at 108 Thornhill Road having plenty of space, we all moved in temporarily while a new conservatory was being added to Petros, with additional redecoration also taking place. In the early hours of December the fifteenth, I arose out of bed to check on Claire, whose diabetes had been very difficult to control since being diagnosed, with early stages of kidney failure and I discovered that Claire was in a coma. This was not a new experience and something that we were used to dealing with, but on this occasion, whether it was Claire's anxiety about her mother, or just sheer bad luck, the glucose injection, which had always worked in the past, failed us and a 999 call was made. I telephoned my nursing daughter Michelle to come immediately to help. When the ambulance arrived and the paramedics decided that she should be hospitalised as soon as possible. Joanne, who was also living in the ground floor flat with Richard, travelled in the ambulance with Claire and Michelle following the ambulance with blue lights flashing, in her own car, while I nervously travelled with Joan to the Manor Hospital for an early morning admission for her mastectomy operation.

On our arrival at the Manor Hospital Walsall admissions ward at 7.45am, I telephoned Dr. Jackson, Claire's specialist at New Cross Hospital Wolverhampton, his secretary made contact with Dr. Jackson, on his mobile phone, to discover that he was still fifteen minutes from the Hospital, and could I call back in twenty minutes?

It seemed like a lifetime as Joan was being prepared for theatre, I re called New Cross and Dr. Jackson took the call immediately. I explained my predicament, Joan in the Manor Hospital awaiting major surgery, Claire in Good Hope Hospital Sutton Coldfield, in a coma. Dr. Jackson said not to worry about Claire, she would recover, but could I arrange to have Claire transferred to him, at New Cross as soon as possible.

I then telephoned Michelle, who was an A&E nurse at Good Hope and asked if she could arrange Claire's transfer to New Cross, she confirmed that it would not be a problem, as the staff there would see it as one less emergency for them to deal with. Joanne travelled with Claire in the ambulance to New Cross and Michelle arrived at the Manor, in time to give encouragement to her mother and together with me, waved the trolley off to theatre, with worry and concern in our hearts and minds.

With Claire's transit to New Cross underway, I travelled from Walsall to meet Dr Jackson, who explained that if the body received too much insulin, it could be stored in the liver and when this happened, although the blood sugar could rebound to normal levels, the patient could remain comatose for between thirty six and forty eight hours, but there would be no lasting damage done. I was reassured with this news and hurried back to the Manor Hospital, to be told that Joan was out of theatre and had been moved into the recovery suite and that the operation had gone well.

In a dazed state Joan returned to the ward where her first though was 'How's Claire?' I gave her Dr. Jackson's explanation and reassured her that she would be fine, as she fell back into an anxious and anaesthetic induced sleep. Michelle and Joanne came to see Mum and I returned to New Cross, where Claire was still in a deep sleep and had not opened her eyes since her admission. I sat by her bedside holding her hand and talking, hoping that she would give me some response.

But I returned home to bed that night, drained and exhausted and still very anxious about two people that were very precious to me and unable to believe that it was still the 15th December and all of this had happened within twenty four hours. I had withstood many pressure situations during my business life, but nothing could have prepared me for a day like that. But I thanked God that night, for the support and help that Joanne and Michelle had been able to give me, on one of the worst days of my life.

The following day was equally hectic as Kate was flying in from Ireland and had to be met at the airport. Firstly, I telephoned New Cross, to hear that Claire had had a comfortable night, but had not recovered consciousness. I also telephoned the Manor Hospital to learn that Joan had also had a comfortable night, stock phrases for ward sisters, but not much help to worried relatives.

Visiting time was two o'clock. I collected Kate from the Airport and with her arrival a united family visited Mum to see her sitting up in bed and although in pain, her only concern was Claire, but she managed a broad smile for Kate, who she had not seen for several weeks. I left Joan with the girls and hurried over to New Cross, to find Claire unchanged and still in a deep sleep. I sought out Dr. Jackson, who again reassured me saying that I must be patient. I returned to Claire's bedside holding her hand again and talking, almost begging for some response, which I could take back to Joan to reassure her, but I left again disappointed. I spent the evening with Joan at the Manor while the girls visited their still comatose sister.

First thing next morning I telephoned New Cross again to be told that Claire had had a comfortable night and although she was not conscious, there were signs that the sleep was more shallow, a shred of comfort at least. Visiting was again shared, the girls going to Mum and I went back to New Cross, to find Claire with her eyes open and although dazed she did recognise me and asked how was Mum, which proved to me that her coma had not impaired either her memory or thinking and was able to tell her that Joan was sitting up and worrying about her.

Dr. Jackson called to see Claire while I was still there, with a broad smile on his face, which almost said 'I told you so'. He asked about Joan and I advised him that the surgery had gone well, but that I did not yet have a post operative prognosis. I exchanged visits with the girls in the evening, they went to New Cross and I went to my best friend and life partner, Joan, who was in some pain, but she had always had a very high pain threshold and just smiled at my concern.

The post operative prognosis indicated that with the complete mastectomy and the removal of eight lymph nodes, they believed that all the cancerous tissue had been removed, but as soon as the wound was sufficiently healed, four courses of chemotherapy would be followed by an extensive course of radiotherapy, then followed by a further four courses of chemotherapy. Whilst they could not give any guarantees that these treatments would pave the way for a complete cure, they were confident that her life would be extended by at least five years.

She could be discharged the next day, if the drain had been removed from her chest. The news from the girls at New Cross was also good; Claire was sitting up with a smile on her face and eating a bite, as the Irish say.

Kate took charge of all of the Christmas shopping and preparations for Mum's return home, Joan was discharged on the 19th December and with much begging with Dr. Jackson, who by now was a personal friend, Claire was given temporary release on Christmas eve, but would have to be readmitted after the Christmas break, as preparations for dialysis would have to be made. Donal, Kate's fiancé flew in from Ireland and Kate cooked a comprehensive Christmas dinner, with all the trimmings. She had to get cross with Joan, who insisted on trying to help despite her discomfort as one arm was totally immobilised. Our Grainger family had all been reunited for a much happier Christmas than had been expected and as the New Year approached, we were all wondering what it would bring.

With the New Year festivities behind us and with Kate staying for an extended holiday to help care for Mum, all of our lives had to return to a different type of normality Joan after the wound healed was facing extensive chemo and radiotherapy and Claire was waiting for admission to hospital for a small operation for a fistula. This is a fairly small surgical procedure to join a vein and an artery in the lower arm in preparation for dialysis.

The operation was made more difficult by Claire's physique, she was small boned and only weighed a little over six stone and had very small veins, as a result the first fistula broke down within a few days and the operation had to be repeated on the upper arm a few weeks later, which was successful.

Claire was spending less time in her own flat now, partly because she felt that she needed more than her own company and partly for her concern for her mother's health and treatment, and she moved back home again, but could still enjoy entertaining her many friends in her own flat when the opportunities arose.

As summer was approaching and most of the family working, the long summer holidays in Ireland were now a thing of the past. With Kate living in the bungalow in Ireland, short regular trips were more common. Michelle and husband Mike decided that Mum would benefit from a break and they booked a cottage in Devon, to suit the best time between chemo treatments. Michelle and Mike set off earlier and had a few days in North Devon exploring Clovelly, Lynton and Lynmouth before meeting up with Joan, Claire and me at the cottage. We had chosen a good few days as the weather was fine and sunny with clear blue skies and a very pleasant holiday ensued with everything going well, with enjoyable day trips and meals in pleasant restaurants, right up until the day before we were due to return, when Joan became ill.

We all raced back up the M5 in convoy, without stopping and went straight to Manor Hospital, a simple blood test revealed that she had an infection and her immune system was at virtually zero. We were given instructions to take Joan straight to the Queen Elizabeth Hospital, where they would be waiting to receive her, 'Don't even stop to collect a tooth brush' we were told. She was quickly admitted to the oncology ward and thankfully with intravenous and a series of additional oral antibiotics she gradually recovered, but a close call had been averted.

Claire was under Dr. Jackson's constant supervision as he wanted to delay dialysis for as long as possible, because when it became necessary, she would have to under go dialysis three days a week for the rest of her life, or until a transplant could be found. Joan gave us all another scare just before the following Christmas after her seventh cycle of chemotherapy, when a thrombosis behind the knee caused her to be hospitalised again.

This was another difficult Christmas, Joan had Christmas dinner in the Manor Hospital, Claire had finally succumbed to dialysis, and I would take her for treatments, now being carried out with three, three hour sessions Monday, Wednesday and Friday each week at Walsall. These treatments were rearranged to avoid Christmas day, which if my memory serves me correctly, fell on a Friday Kate and Donal flew home again and a united family made the best of the prevailing situation. Joan was allowed home after the pulmonary embolism had been treated, but the chemotherapy treatment had taken its toll and as a result, the oncologist would not risk the last chemo treatment because they believed the risks were too high.

With all of the treatment complete, it was six monthly checks and a case of Hail Mary and hope for the best.

Chapter Twenty

Me versus the Revenue

Our anxiety with health problems was increased by a vicious and ill timed letter from the Inland Revenue, stating that they were disagreeing with the worth of various share values relating to the sale of MMF and they made an unbelievable offer of valuation of those shares, which would have resulted in a six figure capital gains tax bill, quite a bombshell on top of all of my other problems. Possibly because of my anger at the timing, or the unpleasant and mischievous nature of the letter, I was driven in to another battle that I was determined not to lose. By this time in my life I was supremely confident in my own ability and drew strength from the fact that I had rarely lost any battle, which I took seriously.

The situation had arisen from good professional advice that I had received from my chartered accountant, Mike Rudd regarding a change in legislation that was about to remove a tax break, that pre April 1999, had protected small company shareholders when they retired and the shares passed to someone else. I should explain that in the eyes of the Revenue, whether or not the shares are gifted, or if they change hands, they would be treated as being sold and a taxable gain could become due. The advice that I had received was to transfer shares into a Discretionary Trust, over which both Joan and I would have complete control and the tax break at that time would be preserved on the value of the shares transferred at that date. It could be interpreted as a legal loophole, but never the less it was legal.

When MMF was sold, I paid all of the capital gains tax that I believed was due for both Joan and me on the difference between the value of the shares when transferred to the Trust and the actual price at which they were sold. The Revenue inspectors were obviously unhappy about the law as it stood and would try with all of the tools at their disposal to claw back any potential revenue that they believed that they could extract. I had already taken steps to offset the gain that my accountant had calculated, by EIS and VCT investments recommended by David Gear. But this new ploy by the Revenue would have had major consequences on those calculations.

Immediately after Christmas, I sent a copy of the revenue letter to Mike and he confirmed that he had heard of this stance being taken with some of his other clients. I was unhappy to hear this news and believed that I should have been warned about the possibility of this situation arising. Mike said not to worry as he would deal with any negotiations with Shares Valuation and believed that he could at least halve the potential liability, but I could see that this could well be a protracted battle, which would rack up heavy professional fees.

I should explain that shares in publicly quoted companies can easily be valued at any time, the value being the mid price quoted at the date in question, but in the case of a privately owned company the value is much more arbitrary, as the share value can vary with how the company is valued at a point in time and the percentage of shares held by any particular shareholder.

I decided to take on the Revenue myself, as I knew the history and the value of the company better than anyone else. I spent many hours reading the IR manuals, which could be accessed online and a three-year battle ensued. Every letter I received from the Revenue, I would immediately re consult all of their manuals, even looking at previous High Court Judgements and then within days would construct ten, twelve and on one occasion fourteen page response, with counter arguments, based on their own manuals. The Revenue officials were duty bound to reply within twenty-one days, which they always adhered to. I kept them under relentless pressure, as every letter I received from them made a better offer to settle than the one before and always with a request for a face to face meeting, for a quick resolution of the differences.

I would respond within days with further arguments, refusing their offer to meet as I knew if we met that at least two experts would arrive from Nottingham, where Shares Valuation are based and as I was learning all the time would have had insufficient time to counter their arguments in a face to face meeting.

My time was free and I was enjoying myself immensely, I could now hardly wait for the next revenue letter to arrive. This was a duel to the end as Mrs. Dorothy Hanson, the official acting for the Revenue, was a specialist in shares valuation and this was her field of expertise, her everyday job. It was not her job to be reasonable. It was her job to get the best settlement for her employer, although the Revenue would dispute this. I quickly realised that I had an enormous advantage, in that I had not employed a professional to argue the case, if I had, there would have been a great temptation to settle at a lower level, to minimise the professional costs that would have been accumulating by the hour, which was a situation that the Revenue was very familiar with and I believe that this was taken into account in their negotiations.

I had weapons of my own, mainly my intimate knowledge of the company and its position in the market place, but also in cases similar to mine, the Revenue would try to minimise the valuation to enable them to raise more of a capital gains tax, on the difference between their valuation at April 1999, when the shares were put into Trust and the eventual price at which they were sold. But contrary to that scenario, if the Revenue were valuing similar shares for inheritance tax purposes, they would attempt to maximise the valuation of the shares and thereby collect more inheritance tax. In fact the IR manuals were very fair, as they had to be, to cover both situations.

My arguments became stronger, as my intimate knowledge of their stance on inherited tax share valuations grew. Minority share holdings were minority share holdings and they could not have one value for inheritance tax and a different value for capital gains tax, although they argued that the manuals were only there for guidance. I argued that their use should and must be consistent. They would not accept any evidence relating to the value of what the shares were eventually sold for, as they claimed that this would have required hindsight, at the valuation date. They would not consider Joan's and my joint shareholding, only as separate entities and argued that a minority holding in a private company had little value, as it could have little influence on decision making in that company. They would not accept that between both of us we held virtually all of the shares. Their arguments were so unfair and unreasonable that an idiot would have found them amusing, but they were based on previous judgements, which the Revenue had managed to obtain in the past.

At this stage I reminded them of the shares that I had purchased from Tony Beard only a few years previous, in fact only months before the shares had been transferred to the Trust. I advised Mrs. Hanson that I had paid £834 each, for just six shares and on this basis alone her arguments were flawed and how could they possible suggest that 468 shares transferred to the Trust, could possibly be worth less than the figure I had paid then.

My tenacity in scouring past cases drew me to Case Law, which revenue officials had brought before the Commissioners, where two named officials had made statements to the Commissioners, relating to valuations based on PE Ratios, which concurred with many of my arguments regarding the way that shares should be valued, in that case concerning an inheritance tax share valuation. The case had a great similarity with my situation, I also discovered a word which was new to my limited vocabulary 'misfeasance' or the misuse of lawful authority, which I then accused the Revenue officials of exactly that.

I had consistently argued that the value of the shares when placed in the Trust were £1200 each, based on the very first BSS offer. The Revenue bombshell Christmas offer had valued them at £235 each which, as previously stated, would have created a huge capital gain, bearing in mind that they had been finally sold for substantially more than my own original valuation.

Mrs. Hanson had reluctantly agreed to raise the Revenue offer to £920 per share and on that basis would I agree to a meeting to bring the matter to a conclusion. I still refused to accept this valuation and the offer to meet, but instead threw another spanner in the works.

I fired my last salvo at Shares Valuation in Nottingham that, now after three years of argument, we were now arguing about pennies, which was not strictly true. Was Mrs. Hanson aware that there was double relief to be taken into the tax calculations? One for the Trust and one for the balance of the shares, I would have been surprised if she did not know, but may not have realised that I also knew, how the final calculations would be made thanks to Terry Lloyd, a Fellow of the Institute of Chartered Tax Accountants, who had given me advice on the method of calculation and it had not been taken into account when I made my original payment for what he believed to be due.

The calculations were very complex and had to take in many considerations, the costs involved in the sale of the company were allowable for tax purposes, retirement relief, EIS and VCT deferral, inflation relief, the second taper relief and the annual relief. As some of the relief was based on percentages it was crucial that they were applied in the correct order to arrive at the correct answer. I knew the correct order and had this all set out on a self calculating spreadsheet and by inserting the current offer from the Revenue into one square I knew exactly what the final result would be and that was how I could tell Mrs. Hanson that I now knew that they were only arguing about pennies. I had already entered the £920 figure on to the spreadsheet and knew that there was virtually nothing due to the Revenue based on that figure.

On receiving my letter, Mrs. Hanson threw the case straight back to the inspector at Wolverhampton, who had brought in Shares Valuation specialist officers to do the dirty work for him over three years earlier. The inspector produced a revised set of calculations, with all of the allowable tax relief included based on the Revenue £920 offer and compared it with my unswerving position of £1200 and invited me to his office to discuss the matter.

In Mr. Pearce's letter he admitted that he had sought expert advice on the method of calculation and had had to make revisions to his earlier calculations. I finally agreed to a meeting, but I told the inspector that he would have to come to me and by this time, bearing in mind that this had been going on for more than three years, and very few Revenue officials were specialised enough to do the calculations correctly and did not have access to my spreadsheet, which by now would do the calculations instantaneously the Revenue wanted shut of Tom Grainger. When the day duly arrived, I invited Mr. Pearce the inspector, into the house, a quite elderly old time inspector with great experience, looking forward to retirement and was probably pleased to be out of the office and racking up some petrol expenses.

Joan hid out of sight in the kitchen and could not believe in my audacity I offered Mr Pearce tea, which he accepted and went on to ask me 'Will you split the difference?' That was the difference between both sides' assessment of what the shares were worth. I was pleasantly surprised and delighted with the offer to value the shares at 3rd April 1999, when they had been transferred to the Trust and a figure of £1050 per share was agreed, as I knew that when all the allowances and reliefs were added to the total overall calculation, the Revenue would owe money to me plus three years' interest. I agreed and within days a letter arrived in the post, confirming their agreement, followed by a cheque for £18,941.46 on the 12th July 2004. A further argument followed in how the interest had been accrued, which I believed had been incorrectly calculated, but that is another story.

Their original demand based on a value of £235 per share had ended up with an agreement at £1050 per share. Would anyone that had my determination and tenacity, plus the IR manuals at their disposal as I had applied over an extended period, ever trust the Inland Revenue if they knew the methods and techniques that they employ to calculate their tax correctly?

The Inland Revenue publish a mission statement and code of conduct that states that they are fair and only want the taxpayer to pay the correct amount of tax that is due, but in my opinion this is pure government propaganda. The legislation is proposed and compiled by Revenue officials and overseen and recommended by the Paymaster General and has been drafted so heavily in their favour that it leaves the taxpayer heavily disadvantaged. It is the only organisation in the UK whereby the taxpayer is guilty unless he can prove himself innocent. They do lose a number of costly court cases each year which are fought at the tax-payer's expense, but if a case is won it enters the statue book and another presided has been created.

CHAPTER TWENTYONE

Joy and Sorrow

Whilst I had been enjoying my skirmishes with the Inland Revenue, my arguments and exchanges had been interspersed with two other battles of a much more serious nature, Joan's struggle with the ravages of an aggressive breast cancer and Claire's deteriorating diabetic condition, which had now progressed and an autonomic neuropathy diagnosis had been confirmed, which meant the diabetes was now affecting part of the nervous system and in turn affecting several other organs. All of Joan's treatment had been completed and the prognosis was good, based on the post treatment checks and generally she felt well and in good form.

Christmas morning arrived and after first Mass and a light breakfast enjoyed with Joanne Jack and Katie, presents were opened and wrapping torn off and thrown in all directions by three excited grandchildren.

Later that year Michelle gave birth to Niamh, which was our fourth grandchild and a sister for Andrew, who was now approaching his third birthday. Joan, I and especially Claire were all very excited about the arrival of the new baby and Claire received another great boost when she heard that there was a possibility of a combined pancreas kidney transplant operation.

Dr. Jackson had written to The Royal Liverpool Hospital referring her case to Professor Sells, an eminent transplant surgeon and he agreed to accept Claire on to the transplant list. We travelled with Claire to The Royal Liverpool Hospital and the procedures and arrangements were outlined and we were given a tour of the transplant suite and it was stressed, at that time, that no patient was in a queue. Patients would be called by the National Transplant Centre based in Bristol and patients would be selected based on the match of the organs that became available and the urgency of the recipient. But if the call came it would be blue lights all the way up the M6 and M62, a pre operative health check and a life changing transplant would be underway.

Claire knew that this was a long shot and a dangerous operation, but it made the dialysis three days a week much more bearable and would be a means to a dream return to the nursing career, to which she was so dedicated. Claire had another appointment with Professor Sells four months later when he advised her that he was concerned that both of her kidneys were badly diseased and he would prefer them to be removed before a transplant was undertaken.

This was a huge set back, but Claire was undeterred and started to put pressure on Dr. Jackson to organise this surgery at the earliest possible date. He was very reluctant, having full knowledge of the dangers of a double nephrectomy for a patient in Claire's condition. Claire was insistent that if this was the only way forward for a transplant, then she wanted to go ahead regardless of the risks for which she was prepared to take full responsibility.

Mr.Weymont, consultant surgeon at New Cross Hospital, reluctantly agreed to perform the operation. We were both very worried, but Claire's determination was an inspiration to us all. The day finally arrived and with hugs and kisses and amid worries we saw her wheeled off for major surgery.

After five hours of waiting and praying, Claire emerged from theatre and was wheeled to the intensive care unit surrounded by four consultants, the consultant anaesthetist who was in charge, Mr Weymont, consultant surgeon, Dr Jackson, renal medical specialist consultant and the diabetic specialist consultant.

Mr. Weymont asked to see us after the operation, which again raised our anxiety levels, as he explained that he had nicked the spleen in the course of the operation, but had repaired it and stopped the bleeding and he did not believe that any lasting damage had been done. We later found that this could have ruled out a transplant if this had gone wrong.

Three days later Claire sat up in bed, back on the main ward and said 'Well I'm better off without them useless kidneys anyway,' adding 'I feel great, bring on the transplant'. In the next bed was her sister Joanne, who had a kidney stone removed the day before and was feeling very sick from the anaesthetic, but was discharged a few days later, while Claire stayed on in ward 18 having to undergo dialysis sessions until she was fit to return as an out patient.

After she had fully recovered from the surgery, we returned with Claire to Liverpool and Professor Sells said how pleased he was that the operation had gone so well and she was back on the transplant list, however, without any kidneys, the diabetes was almost impossible to control. I would check Claire who was now living back in Middleton Road at 3am every morning to ensure she was not in a coma and it was not uncommon that she was, or had a very low blood sugar count, but a glucagon injection would usually solve the problem within twenty minutes.

The diabetic specialist recommended an insulin pump to help with the blood sugar control, but the Primary Health Care Trust would not fund the pump, or the ongoing costs of maintaining its use. I wrote to Richard Shepherd MP for Aldridge and Brownhills and went on to meet him, armed with all of the medical documents and recommendations and within twelve weeks the PCT agreed to fund the pump.

While Claire was having dialysis in Walsall, an opportunity arose for an exchange with a patient who was undergoing dialysis in Truro in Cornwall, who wanted to visit a friend in Walsall. This was a rare opportunity and was quickly snapped up by Claire, as holidays now were a major logistical undertaking, with treatment being necessary on alternate days. We booked a hotel in Newquay, which overlooked Fistral Bay. The dialysis times had been arranged at the Royal Cornwall Hospital in Truro, for six o'clock in the evening on Monday, Wednesday and Friday and the rest of the time was free for a Cornish holiday in the sun. Trips to The Eden Project, Penzance, Polperro, and Falmouth were among many of the highlights of our holiday. The hotel staff saved meals for Claire and I until we returned after each three hour dialysis session, before enjoying the evening entertainment in the ballroom and retiring to bed.

Christmas 2003 brought sensational and unexpected news to all of us, we were all gathered together for the festive season, Kate and Donal had flown in from Ireland and after a Christmas shopping spree, we were all sitting down to Christmas eve dinner, always a special menu, pre organised with much thought and usually orchestrated by Claire, when as if by magic, Kate displayed a sparkling engagement ring and announced that Millstreet Church had been booked and the Castlerosse Hotel in Killarney had been also been booked for a 21st July 2004 wedding, the joy and excitement that this news brought gave us all a much needed lift in spirits.

No one is quite sure why everyone was so surprised at the engagement, because Kate and Donal had been dating each other while still at school, in fact I first met the groom to be, when he came to England for Kate's debs ball just before she left school to start University and now, nearly a decade later, they were at last planning their wedding.

Soon after Christmas, the arrangements for Kate's wedding were in full swing and she flew over from Ireland with Geraldine O'Leary who was to be bridesmaid with Claire and a weekend of fittings of dresses, tiaras, shoes and accessories followed. This was a short stay for Kate and Geraldine, but none the less it was very enjoyable, with all of the pre nuptial excitement and was brought to an end with an excellent meal at the Boat House Restaurant in Sutton Park. Throughout the weekend, Claire was concerned whether she would be well enough to carry out her role as a bridesmaid between dialysis sessions in Ireland, but Kate's encouragement left her in no doubt that she would be fine.

Claire's health care was now very time consuming, but she was always upbeat and such a pleasure to care for, that it never seamed like a task or duty, but the dialysis was causing a calcium build up in her veins, first in her toes, then her fingers and even when she had a toe removed she said, 'I don't care if they take my foot off, as long as I get that transplant.' She was such an amazing young lady, never complaining, never looking back and could always see a future for herself and a determination to overcome whatever the good Lord threw at her. With all of the set backs over many years, I never once hear her said 'Why Me?'

On the 15th April 2004 after a consultant group case conference, it was decided to perform a skin graft to relieve a calcium build up on her hip. Again the operation went well and on the 18th April we were both visiting as usual between 6pm to 8pm and at 8.15, she waved us goodbye with a broad smile and her last words, 'Don't forget my toast for dialysis in the morning Dad.' At 00.15 on the 19th we received the called we had always feared. Claire had had a heart attack. We raced back to Ward 18 New Cross Hospital, but by the time we were allowed to see her, it was too late. The staff had worked tirelessly to revive her, but she was gone from us, a marathon battle against all of the odds had finally been lost.

Our four beloved girls were now only three, but that's far from being true, because Claire's memories, her radiant smile, her courage, her determination, her care as a nurse and the memories of a warm kind and loving daughter and sister, would live on for ever in all of our minds.

We were all were obviously devastated, Claire had been seriously ill for many years, but her will to fight and live had seemed to make her indestructible. Joan had lost a soul mate that she could empathise with about her own worries if the cancer should return, Joanne had her own partner Richard, Michelle was married and had her own family, and Kate was living in Ireland and I was a man and this combination created a very special relationship between Claire and Joan as female kindred spirits.

I had become very close to Claire, every parent loves all of their children, but special situations arise that build special relationships. That had happened with Claire and me. Starting early Monday, Wednesday and Friday for dialysis in Walsall, when every day Westlife's version of Uptown Girl would blast the airways at least twice as we drove to Walsall, and a further weekly appointment with Dr. Jackson at New Cross Hospital gave us both ample opportunities for us to talk about our targets, ambitions, and any concerns about the family. Claire always worried far more about her mother's cancer than she did about her own health, but these were special opportunities for us to talk to each other, an opportunity some families never get. She told me that she was far more worried about living, especially if anything happened to her Mum and Dad, than she was about dying. She had always had a great affinity with her grandfather, my Dad, and she was unswervingly sure that he was waiting in Heaven for her if the transplant was unsuccessful. But I had now lost my Uptown Girl.

Joanne and Michelle had both lost a sister who they had grown up with and shared twenty nine years, exchanging secrets about school, boyfriends and all manner of happy and sad times. Joanne had built a special relationship when they shared flats at Thornhill Road, when her husband Ken had walked out and had left Joanne with two lovely children Jack four and Katie only a few months old. Ken's desertion had left Joanne very depressed for several months and Claire was an ideal person to love, care for and encourage Joanne, assuring her that things could only get better. Michelle's grief was deeper, she and Claire had always loved Ireland and they had a similar soft personality streak, undoubtedly inherited from Joan. Michelle was also a very deep thinker and would try to analyse details, even things which were beyond scrutiny.

Kate, who lived permanently in Ireland, was hurt by Claire's death, she felt that she had not been kept up to date about how ill Claire was, but in truth, the family around Claire had all become complacent that throughout all of the many crises that Claire had gone through, she always came back larger than life and with a greater determination to lead a normal life. It had seemed impossible that she could die. Kate and Claire had shared the same bed as children, being the two youngest, they had both loved Ireland, the Irish lads and freedom of life, and now Kate had not only lost a sister that she deeply loved, but her bridesmaid for her wedding in three months time. Such a joyous occasion, now dampened by a huge hole, that such a special person had left behind.

St. Anne's Church was bursting at the seams for Claire's funeral, many school friends came from far and near, colleagues from work, many friends and relations travelled from Ireland, nurses from the dialysis unit and many of my Catenian friends who knew Claire from social functions, all came to pay tribute to the passing of a very exceptional and brave young lady.

A poem, which fell into my hands on a scrap of paper and at the time I had no idea who the author was, but it's so profound that I hope the originator will allow me to use it to illustrate our feelings at this time.

'I'll lend you for a little while, a child of mine God said.

'For you to love the while she lives and mourn for when she's dead.

'It May be six or seven years or twenty two or three,

'But will you, till I call her back, take care of her for me?

'She'll bring her charms to gladden you and should her stay be brief,

'You'll all ways have her memories as a source for all your grief.

'I cannot promise she will stay, since all from earth return,

'But there are lessons taught below I want this child to learn.

'I've looked the whole world over, in my search for nurses true,

'And from folks that crowd life's lane, I have chosen you.

'Now will you give her all your love, nor think the labour vain,

'Nor hate me when I come to take this lent child back again.

'I fancied that I heard them say 'Dear Lord thy will be done,

'For all the joys thy child will bring, the risks of grief we'll run.

'We'll shelter her with tenderness, we'll lover her while we may,

'And for the happiness we've known, for ever grateful stay,

'But should the Angels call her, much sooner than we've planned,

'We'll brave the bitter grief that comes, and try to under stand.'

Much later I learned that that the poem was written by Edger L. Guest and is entitled 'God's lent child.'

Life had to go on and everyone was determined that Kate's marriage to Donal Twomey should be the great day that Claire would have wanted above all else. The ceremony again was to follow our footsteps up the aisle of St. Patrick's Church Millstreet

This wedding was to be even more of a logistical challenge than Michelle's had been, in so much as we had invited our own Parish Priest, Fr.Gwil Lloyd to officiate, who like me was a convert from the Methodist Church, a priest ordained a Catholic Priest after marrying his wife Jenny. A married Priest in Millstreet, in fact in Ireland, was unusual to say the least. Fr. Gwill on seeing the church thought it was more like a Cathedral and was a little over awed at what he had taken on. However, he was reassured, when I told him that Fr. Paddy, a relation of Donal's, was home from Nebraska and would be assisting him with the Nuptial Mass.

Our English guests were all booked into local B&Bs for the night and then Castlerosse Hotel following the reception, as there was still no suitable hotels in Millstreet.

We had arranged for our English guests and close friends and relatives to meet up for a buffet and drinks in Lal's Bar the evening before the wedding, we thought that this would be easier than repeating the buffet in the bungalow of five years previous for Michelle's wedding.

The following day started early, first with the hairdresser and beautician, followed by the photographer and video man recording the pre-nuptial preparations in the bungalow, with four very excited grandchildren posing for photographs. The morning sped by and a cream vintage 1921 Durant Star, driven by a replica of Parker from Thunderbirds arrived at the bungalow to convey a Kate Moss look-alike, Kate Grainger on my arm to her betrothed.

The church was bathed in sunshine when we arrived and as we composed ourselves before the long walk up the aisle to the music of Rosie and Derry Healey, a husband and wife instrumental and vocal duo I gave Kate a wink, or was it a tear, at the thought of handing my baby over to another man. The Nuptial Mass was beautifully concelebrated by Fr. Gwill and Fr. Paddy and broadcast to the whole of Millstreet by closed circuit television. The register was signed and with more photographs taken, the convoy drove off to Killarney, again with horns blaring and lights flashing, arriving at the Castlerosse Hotel to the waiting local press photographer and champagne.

The venue was a building of Chateau design overlooking a golf course, which formed a panoramic front lawn leading to the banks of Lough Leane with Macgillycuddy Reeks in the background, a truly magnificent setting for a splendid occasion, which was enhanced with excellent cuisine accompanied by good wine. The speeches were of a very high standard and amusing, with everyone in good form for an evening of music and dance that carried on unbounded well into the early hours of the following day.

After all of the excitement was over we reflected that all of our four girls were now settled, Kate was now Mrs. Twomey, Claire at home in Heaven with her idolised

Granddad Grainger, although sadly missed, Joanne with Richard, and Michelle with Michael and family. Would they enjoy their thirty-eight years together, as much as we had; only time would tell?

We returned home to a house that had seen so many changes since we had bought it over thirty five years ago. But it was a house without Claire and although Claire's death had released us from a round the clock caring role, I always felt an element of guilt when I travelled, especially to Ireland that I was going without her and always with the special van trip that we had shared together clearly in my mind.

A little after Kate and Donal's first wedding anniversary, Kate was able to broadcast the news that she was pregnant and expecting her first baby. The 27th August 2005 arrived bringing baby Adam into the world to great excitement, although he gave us all a scare, when he had an epileptic fit soon after birth, our fifth grandchild and another boy joined the world amid many celebrations. We spent another happy holiday in the bungalow, with daily hospital visits to coo over and cuddle to our newest grandson.

Our girls were busy organising a big party as we were due to celebrate the fortieth anniversary of our marriage. The 14th October 2005 would mark a milestone in that journey of love and devotion, a voyage that had seen many changes in fortune and many great joys and inevitably some sorrows.

Joanne had booked my local golf club for the venue; all of our friends were invited friends both past and present, some travelling long distances to share this special occasion with us. After an enjoyable meal Joanne very nervously made a very moving speech, to which

I responded thanking everyone for coming and for the part that all of their friends had contributed to our unique relationship together. This was followed by a further celebration in Ireland again at the Castlerosse Hotel with Joan's family who were not able to travel to the English celebration.

A short time later we were helping to tidy Claire's old flat at in Thornhill Road when we found a sealed letter written by Claire, simply addressed to 'My Family'. The letter was undated, but I believe that it was written prior to the major surgery for the removal of her kidneys. Its contents would have moved any reader to tears, as it expressed in very simple terms her undying gratitude to us for the love and care throughout her life and her wealth of joy that her sisters and extended family had brought to her life. There were also bequests to her nieces and nephews. Small children that she would dearly have borne herself, but sadly she was never afforded that opportunity.

An amazing coincidence had occurred when we had bought our house in Middleton Road all those years ago, in that our neighbours were also called Tom and Joan, but they were brother and sister and had moved into their house many years before we bought our house. They were well into their eighties when tragedy struck, late one evening, when a tap on the front door revealed a distraught Joan Hawley, saying the she thought that her brother had died.

I hurried next door to find my good friend and neighbour, Tom Hawley half in and half out of bed, clearly lifeless. I passed the news on to my wife Joan and she consoled the deceased's sister, while

I telephoned for the Priest and a doctor, followed by a call to Bill Harris, Joan Hawley's brother in law who lived nearby.

After Tom Hawley's funeral, Joan, together with Joan Hawley's sister and nieces did their best to console a very distressed and depressed elderly lady, but fighting a faltering battle against loneliness, she eventually succumbed to requests from a worried family and very reluctantly moved into a Nursing Home in Walsall. Her home of over forty years was to be sold. We called to see our long time neighbour in the Nursing Home and the transformation was astounding, whether it was being away from the years of old memories, or whether it was the care, company and TLC, we did not know, but we were greeted by a smartly dressed and alert Joan, who was brimming with news of how pleased she was with the care she was receiving and how confused some of the other old patients were.

I made an offer to buy the empty and neglected house next door, with two objectives firstly to have control over who my next neighbour would be, but also with a view to my next project extending and refurbishing the property. A price was agreed between JMCK Properties and the nieces and nephews, who were to inherit the property and were organising their aunt's health care and we completed the purchase without employing an agent.

I arranged for plans to be drawn up by a chartered engineer, which were duly submitted for planning approval and after many changes due to the house being situated in a conservation area, planning permission for the extensions at the side and rear was eventually granted for an extensive two storey extension.

As Christmas was approaching and almost five years to the day, we learned that Joan's breast cancer had returned, devastating news bringing memories of chemotherapy and radiotherapy engraved on our minds. We were told that Joan would require further surgery, which was to be performed within two weeks in December. After the operation we were led to believe that the surgery had been successful, but she would require plastic surgery early in January, as the wound left by the surgical procedure would not heal on its own.

January 2006 brought a ray of sunshine to all of our hearts, when on the first day of the New Year Liam Smyth entered the world via his mother's work place, Good Hope Hospital and being the first baby of the New Year, he was an instant celebrity in the local papers. Liam was our sixth grandchild, a bonny little lad and he helped to brighten up our hopes for the New Year, after a festive season that had been steeped in worry about Joan's prognosis.

The plastic surgery was performed by a specialist in Sandwell Hospital, but the evening following the surgery, the surgeon telephoned me full of apologies, advising me that he had been miss informed as to the state of the cancer and whilst he had done his best with the plastic surgery, he believed that more treatment would be required. In retrospect the tone of this conversation and profuse apologies really served notice of the beginning of the end, and although Joan had been told that she would require further surgery for the cancer, it was not necessary for her to convey the bad news to me.

An appointment was made to see a top plastic and thoracic surgeon privately, who subject to tests, would remove two ribs and perform deep surgery on the intercostal muscle and the operation would be performed at the Queen Elizabeth Hospital, where Joan had had all of our babies. However a full body scan detected two secondary tumours, one in the right upper breast and a small one in the liver. The specialist surgeon said that it was unwise to put Joan through such major surgery, when it would still leave the secondary tumours untreated. We both knew the gravity of this news but could not find any words of comfort for each other, both trying to believe that the other may not know that hopes for the future were fading.

Joan was referred back to Dr. Fernando the oncologist and another course of chemotherapy was programmed, to be followed by more radiotherapy, but by now Joan was desperately trying to conceal how much pain she was experiencing. After the chemotherapy had been completed, and she was now into a further course of radiotherapy, which was the cause of one particularly bad week, having to travel to the QE two days running, first for a bone scan, which caused her much discomfort and the following day a marathon trip for radiotherapy, which ended in failure when a heavy snow fall brought the City to a standstill and having left home at three o'clock in the afternoon, for what should have been a two hour round trip, turned into six hours of endurance and no treatment.

Whenever the first fall of snow comes, it never fails to bring Birmingham and other major cities to a standstill. The surprise that snow falls in the winter is unbounded to the Highways Agency, but if they had personal experience of the pain and suffering that the disruption to emergency services brings, maybe, just maybe, they could do things differently.

The wound which had resulted from the surgery almost a year earlier, had been treated daily by community nurses Sue and Jackie mainly who were two very nice and very caring people and throughout their many visits, a special relationship was established and they became part of the family, sharing our concerns and disappointments.

Joan's condition was clearly deteriorating and a further appointment with Dr Fernando confirmed the blood cancer level was rising and he recommended further oral chemotherapy. This gave us some hope that the cancer could be repelled. Despite all off the signs our determination to fight for something so precious was insatiable. Kate came home with baby Adam and did her best to keep all our flagging spirits up. The community nurses were clearly less hopeful, although they did nothing to suppress our hopes, but they did arrange for Melanie a specialist nurse from St. Giles' Hospice, to call to help with the pain relief treatment.

Joan's birthday arrived 6th February and we travelled to Tamworth for a short mooch around the shops and coffee and a cake in Drucker's, but the fact that Joan would only share some of my cake indicated that she was feeling pretty poorly, because she was mad about Drucker's cakes when she was well. The following week, Michelle took Joan to a nearby nursery knowing Joan's love of the garden and flowers and she bought her gardening gloves and other presents, which were never used.

The oral chemo was not winning the battle and Melanie started preparing us all for Joan's death, as Joan would get up from bed less and less and the morphine got stronger and stronger.

I prepared a chart on a spreadsheet to monitor the morphine dosage, just for something to do really, hoping that I could make some difference and to try to overcome my feeling of hopelessness. Joan made one last super human effort to get dressed to keep an appointment with Dr. Fernando at nearby Little Aston Hospital, as she was determined not give up, mainly for me, but also for Kate who was expecting another baby in July and she was determined, regardless of anything else, that she wanted to see Kate's new baby.

But this visit to hospital took super human effort and determination that would not be matched by any other living soul, when she arrived at the entrance she swept aside any idea of a wheelchair and gritted her teeth as she walked the long corridor to the waiting room as she would not show the doctor how ill she was. Dr. Fernando gave me the name of a liver specialist who had developed a special radiotherapy treatment for liver cancer. After seeing the agonising effort that Joan had made to get dressed and keep the hospital appointment, I did not believe that she could take much more and when I telephoned the specialist I asked, 'Can you cure her?' His reply was No, but he could control the pain.

I made the most difficult decision of my life and refused the treatment, I knew it was comparable to with switching off a life support machine, but the pain was being controlled and I loved Joan too much to let her endure an impossible trip to the QE Hospital. I had to let go of my best friend, my soul mate, my rock, and my love of a lifetime.

Joan's family in Ireland had been kept in touch with the situation and as time drew near Dennis and Nora flew over, but Joan now heavily sedated, just about recognised and acknowledged them. Two nights later, I preyed that the Lord would reunite Joan with our daughter Claire and at 6am the following morning. 27th March 2007, with all of her sombre family round her, this very special, gentle, dignified lady slipped peacefully away from us.

THE END

EPILOGUE

Life after Death

Most of us old timers have already experienced the devastation that the death of a loved one brings and for the young, the mere thought of Mum, Dad or a brother or sister dying is a thought that is almost beyond comprehension.

My own experiences are still vivid in my memory, the loss of two very special people within a few years, each bringing a sadness and an emptiness, that the loss of something precious brings, the infinitive thought that I would never in my lifetime see these loved ones again. The clichés 'Time is a great healer,' and 'Life must go on,' are well meant but sounded very hollow when the initial despair was upon me.

But a lifetime of happy events and things that we did together, meeting Joan, our engagement, our wedding, the joy that the birth of our four daughters brought, seeing them develop, first tooth, first steps, and the mixed emotions as they each entered that first day at school. Holidays, mainly to county Cork seeing the children help about the farm. The horse riding and ice skating that we enjoyed together and seeing and remembering Joan's influence as they developed into young ladies and the shared excitement as they trained for their chosen careers, their weddings and the arrival of grandchildren. This multitude of happy memories and experiences are all the things that enhance life after death for us that are left behind, because all of these happy memories and times are just as infinite and vivid as the stark emotions that the death of loved ones bring.

As the book has portrayed, there were the inevitable set backs, when Joanne was diagnosed diabetic at only ten years of age and then Claire when she was 15, which was later to prove so catastrophic, leading eventually to renal and heart failure and her death at the age of 29. But again, Claire's 29 years brought me great joy, and her courage through years of dialysis and a determination to be fit enough for a transplant are emblazoned on my memory with pride.

Joan's cancer was a tragedy for all of us, but her deep faith gave us hope and that same faith has always been a very powerful influence on all of our lives. Firstly in my conversion to Catholicism and secondly Joan's appointment as one of the first two female Eucharistic Ministers at St. Anne's Church, a change that was not universally welcomed at the time has now been vindicated, as female Eucharistic Ministers and Servers are widely accepted.

In addition the legacy has left me with three surviving daughters, two of their husbands and eight grandchildren all practicing Catholics. I'm also sure that she looks down proudly on her three eldest grandchildren serving on the alter at first Mass and would know that her example had played its part in their wanting to become Servers. I am equally sure that as my other grandchildren each receive their First Holy Communion, they will also be inspired by her faith and presence in the church.

When Joan was alive we always attended 8.30 Mass together for over forty years at St Anne's Church. Fr. O'Healy was the first Priest to welcome us to the Parish and was the first Priest to visit our home. He also baptised all four girls. Sadly Fr. O'Healy died the day that the Pope landed in England for his first visit to the country on 28th May 1982. Since Joan's loss in March 2007, the 8.30 Mass on Sunday has been a high priority for me, as I can still feel her presence and the many memories of our family occupying a full pew for ourselves are further examples of life after death for the living.

Life after death is as definite as the depth of our own personal faith and the yearning and belief that I will one day, be reunited with my loved ones, together with the happy times and memories that helps to sustain me through the many difficult times without them.

* * * * * *

I continued extending and modernising the house next door with the help of Andy, Ron Gerrard's son in law, and the project kept me busy while mourning the loss of my soul mate, the project was completed by autumn 2008.

Our family has remained very close and my two daughters who live nearby are inspired by Joan's example and have done their best to take her place. I was diagnosed with bladder cancer in September 2008, which was treated with surgery, chemotherapy and radiotherapy and rekindled many of my earlier memories with Joan's treatment. I am currently clear of cancer and feel fit and well. I still make regular trips to Ireland to see the progress that Kate and Donal are making with the construction of their own house about three miles from the bungalow, which gave all of us so much pleasure, over many years.

Jackie, the community nurse that cared for Joan for more than a year, still keeps a watchful eye on me and we enjoy the occasional meal together.

Joanne still works for MMF as credit controller and the company continues to grow and thrive, with Terry McIvor, operations director working more time from home in Cornwall, and John Hornby sales director due to retire this year.

Kate gave birth to her sister's namesake, a healthy girl, Claire Elizabeth on the 4th July 2007 less than three months after the loss of Joan. Ron Gerrard and I went to Ireland to baby sit Adam for the duration of the birth, which had its humorous moments when us two old codgers took Adam with us for a meal and had to get help with the baby chair, which had old deckchair connotations. Another milestone was created when I changed my first ever nappy when Adam left me with a little present.

Michelle and Michael added my eighth grandchild, Evelyn Smyth on the 25th March 2008, who is now walking and talking her own language that only her brother Liam understands. She is a delight to me and we are mad about each other.

I still value Ron Gerrard's friendship, which continues to grow with Ron's failing eye sight having been helped enormously by St. Dunstan's, who have added a new dimension to his life and a recent holiday in the Yorkshire Dales and Lake District preceeded the devastating floods in Cockermouth in Cumbria by one week. My luck is still holding out.

Selkirk UK went into liquidation in 2004 and was taken over by SFL Flues and Chimneys and continues to manufacture in Barnstaple, North Devon. The original Selkirk Metalbestos LLB was bought by Thomkins plc and re-entered the flue market through agreements with Deks Distribution UK in 2006 and an old name from the past David Jones still continues to sell flue systems for them.

Rite Vent Ltd. was taken over by Schiedel and still operates from Washington, County Durham.

Lightning Source UK Ltd.
Milton Keynes UK
24 September 2010

160309UK00001B/4/P